Spirituality
and
Self-Empowerment

Spirituality
and
Self-Empowerment

HOW TO OPEN UP YOUR MAGICAL, MYSTICAL MIND POWER

Gloria Chadwick

CONTEMPORARY
BOOKS
A TRIBUNE NEW MEDIA COMPANY

Library of Congress Cataloging-in-Publication Data

Chadwick, Gloria.
    Spirituality and self-empowerment : how to open up
your magical, mystical mind power / Gloria Chadwick.
        p.   cm.
    ISBN 0-8092-3441-6
    1. Spiritual life.   2. Success.   I. Title.
    BL624.C4   1995
    291.4—dc20   95-32765
                                                    CIP

Copyright © 1995 by Gloria Chadwick
All rights reserved
Published by Contemporary Books, Inc.
Two Prudential Plaza, Chicago, Illinois 60601-6790
Manufactured in the United States of America
Printed on recycled paper
International Standard Book Number: 0-8092-3441-6
10   9   8   7   6   5   4   3   2   1

This book is dedicated to the philosopher.
Thanks for sharing your knowledge and for
journeying with me on the rainbow path.

Contents

Introduction

It's been said that we use only 10 percent of our mind. Since I was curious about the other 90 percent, I decided to look inside my mind to see if I could find out what's really there. Twenty-two years ago, I embarked on a journey of self-discovery. I read thousands of books, attended hundreds of classes and workshops, and spent a lot of time within my thoughts, feelings, dreams, and imagination. Somewhere along the way, I began exploring my experiences from the inside out.

The most important thing I learned is that we already know everything about our true spiritual nature; we've just forgotten how to remember and apply our inner knowing in our lives. The purpose of this book is to help you bring forth the knowledge already inside you, to help you empower yourself and open yourself up to your spiritual essence. It's my way of sharing what I rediscovered and is a composite of the classes I've taught on positive mind power and psychic/spiritual awareness for the past eleven years.

Spirituality and Self-Empowerment offers you many ways to open up, explore, experience, and understand the natural power of your mind. This book can serve as a guide or a beginning point to help you build an avenue of awareness between your conscious and subconscious minds, between the everyday and the awesome. It offers you a journey into a special place within yourself where you can rediscover your inner knowledge and reawaken your true spiritual nature.

The text, visualizations, and meditations will guide you step by step into the magical, mystical power of your mind. It's just like breathing. Before you know it, you'll realize that you're truly a spiritual being and you'll remember what you've always known. It's as if you're waking up from a dream and discovering that the dream is real.

This book is written in a hands-on, how-to format that encourages you to explore and experience both the physical and spiritual sides of yourself—to open up and apply the power of your mind in a way that's most meaningful for you. You'll find a few teachy-type lectures and more than a few questions without answers. You'll also come across mind-opening meditations and Mind-Power Exercises interspersed throughout the book.

You are your own best teacher, and your experiences will teach you lessons. Just like in school, there are homework assignments at the end of each chapter, but don't let this deter you or dampen your spirits—they're fun to do and will show you many magical things within yourself. You don't even have to *do* them. Just by thinking about them, you'll be "doing them" on another level in your mind.

The exercises and meditations are a general guide; feel free to change them to suit your lifestyle and to fit your frame of awareness. Just follow your feelings. You'll know if something is right for you—if it resonates within your mind. If something doesn't interest you or appeal to you, look into why. It may be something that doesn't relate to you right now or it may be something you've already accomplished. Then again, it might be exactly what you need to experience at this moment in time; it might be something that could turn out to be very helpful.

Just as you would begin a physical exercise program with simple stretches and easy exercises, and you'd exercise every day to condition and strengthen yourself, so it is with exercising your mental muscles. Begin with a gentle stretching and limbering of your mind and your imagination. As you exercise and strengthen the magical power of your mind, you'll begin to condition and redevelop your natural mystical abilities.

As you explore the magic inside your mind, you'll be opening up very powerful energies. Part I—Self-Empowerment is designed to help you reestablish a positive pattern of thinking, feeling, and acting as you redevelop the magical power of your mind. Part II—Spirituality is designed to help you energize and revitalize your mystical abilities as you realize your full potential as a spiritual being.

Opening up the power of your mind requires quiet time to listen to your thoughts and feelings every day. Learning more about yourself and your physical nature is a prelude to clearly understanding your spiritual nature. This is a process, and it takes time to bring your subconscious knowing into your conscious thoughts. It takes time to go within to find your own answers and to explore your experiences in every level of your awareness. As you spend the time within your thoughts, feelings, dreams, and imagination, you'll find yourself richly rewarded as you explore and develop and really understand the most wonderful resource you possess . . . your mind.

Spirituality
and
Self-Empowerment

Part I
Self-
Empowerment

Ready to take a wonderful mind trip—
a journey into the magical, mystical
power of your mind, where you can
follow a rainbow path to open up,
explore, and rediscover all that is
within you and reawaken to your
true spiritual self?

CHAPTER ONE

Relaxation and Rainbows

Before you do anything else, take off your shoes and relax. Sit in a comfortable chair and settle in with a pencil, paper, and crayons. Now, draw a picture of a rainbow and color it in using the seven natural colors of a rainbow— red, orange, yellow, green, blue, indigo (a deep purplish- blue), and violet. Look at your rainbow. What's your favorite color? Get inside your feelings about your favorite color. Explain why it's your favorite color and how it makes you feel. Save your description; you'll be using it later.

That wasn't such hard work, was it? Opening up the magical power of your mind is going to be fun and easy; all you have to do is relax, color rainbows, and describe your feelings about your favorite color. And one more thing. I want you to breathe. Take a deep breath and begin to relax even more completely. Put your crayons away and get comfy. Wiggle around in your chair and breathe some more. Read through the following relaxation suggestions, then close your eyes and get into the rhythm of relaxing. If you already have a relaxation method that you use and like, go with your own method. But try this one at least once to see how you feel about it.

Take a deep breath and begin to feel a sense of relaxation that flows through your body, beginning at the top of your head. Imagine it as a gentle wave of feeling that flows softly through you, descending gradually and slowly through your forehead and your face, down into your neck and your shoulders.

Let this wonderful feeling of relaxation flow down through your arms, elbows, hands, and fingers, gently easing all the tension, letting it drift away, replacing it with a soft, natural feeling of relaxation that flows all the way down through your back, vertebra by vertebra, loosening all the tension and tightness.

Maybe you'd like to move around a bit; readjust your position and get even more comfortable. Take a moment to stretch and then relax even more deeply, now that you've let go of all the tightness and tension from your neck, shoulders, and back.

Sinking deeper into your comfortable chair, you notice that your breathing slows to a deep and regular rhythm

as the gentle feeling of relaxation flows easily and natu-
rally down through your chest and abdomen. You feel so
deeply relaxed. Peaceful. Quiet. Soothed, as the feeling of
relaxation continues to flow gently down through your
hips and thighs, through your knees, calves, ankles, feet,
and toes. You're so comfortable and relaxed, feeling per-
fectly in tune with yourself. Enjoy your feeling of relax-
ation for a while. Just breathe and be happy. Enjoy the
*warm, pleasant feeling of just **being**.*

There's an art to relaxing your body and it's easy to do.
As you take a few deep breaths, you cleanse your lungs
and begin to clear your mind. As you're breathing in,
imagine that you're inhaling positive, relaxing feelings. As
you're breathing out, imagine that you're exhaling negative thoughts and feelings, letting go of all cares, worries,
or problems, releasing your thoughts from your everyday
experiences. As you allow a feeling of relaxation to replace
tension, you allow all the muscles and nerves and tissues,
and every part of your body, to relax, from the top of your
head all the way down through the tips of your toes.

As your body becomes more relaxed, you begin to tune
out the physical, conscious level for a time, and you enter
a more subtle, aware, subconscious level as you direct
your attention inward. When you first begin to relax and
open up your inner awareness, you may experience conscious chatter. "Conscious chatter" is merely a distraction
that goes something like this: "Omigod, I forgot to go to

the dentist. Work was awful and it's going to be even worse tomorrow. I should call so-and-so, and I have to do this, that, and the other, etc., so on and so forth"—just chatter, mostly about mundane matters—everyday information that you can listen to when you're not centering your attention on discovering the magic of your mind. If this happens, gently focus your awareness on your breathing. Allow your breathing to relax you and help you quiet the chatter as you direct your attention inward.

By relaxing and allowing your conscious mind to become calm and quiet, physical changes occur within your body that relate directly to your health and well-being. You reduce and eliminate stress, tension, and fatigue. Your breathing and heart rate slow to a natural, peaceful rhythm, and your internal organs are affected in a gentle, healing way. Your digestive system and nervous system calm themselves. As you relax even more deeply, your body releases endorphins and hormones, which increase your feelings of physical and mental well-being. Your brain waves slow from a Beta rhythm, which is your normal, waking, conscious level, to an Alpha rhythm, which is a more aware subconscious level of mind.

By tuning out conscious thoughts and worries, you're turning your attention inward toward your subconscious mind. This is very important as you begin to explore your mind and exercise your mental muscles. If, while you're relaxed, a thought that sounds like conscious chatter runs through your mind, just watch it run by; let it drift in and out. Gently ignore it and it will go away. Some thoughts can interfere in Alpha when they belong in Beta. If it's important for you to be aware of it right now, it'll sit there in the center of your mind and make faces at you until you pay attention to it.

As you enter a more aware level of mind, you enjoy many benefits of opening up and expanding your inner awareness. You create and enjoy a more positive attitude and a better frame of mind. You open a channel of communication between your conscious and subconscious minds that will help you in any way you desire. You open your receptivity to ideas and insights, which in turn influence your intuition and creativity. You open avenues of self-discovery and expression. You open yourself up to exploring the magical power of your mind and to experiencing your natural abilities of mystical awareness.

Relaxing, opening up your mind, and focusing your attention and awareness inward is a natural, flowing process. Your subconscious is like a bud that's growing into a very beautiful flower. Allow it to grow at its own rate. Nurture it with care and loving attention. As a bud, it needs time to develop and flourish—to flower and bloom and grow into a very beautiful garden.

The following mind-opening meditation is a visualization to help you gently stretch your mind and your imagination. You'll be exploring the energies of the seven colors of a rainbow by experiencing the vibrations of each color, by seeing and feeling what they represent to you on an inner level. Read through the meditation first to see what it says, then close your eyes and experience it. If you'd prefer, you can make a recording of it to listen to while you relax into the rainbow, or you can have someone read the meditation to you.

As you ascend through all the colors in the rainbow, take your time inside each color to completely enjoy and experience and absorb the color within your body and your mind. Breathe the colors inside you. See and feel and sense the vibrations and energies of each color as you go inside and through the magical, mystical rainbow in your mind.

As you go inside each color, allow yourself to see an image or an object of that color. Clearly visualize the image; see the thought of it in your mind. The thought itself will draw a picture for you. Perhaps you'll see a scene involving several images that move and change as you become more aware of them. Accept the first thing you see. Your subconscious speaks to you in symbols and imagery; it's the language of your mind. By accepting the pictures that your mind offers you, you'll be opening a channel of communication between your subconscious and conscious minds. The images you see and the feelings you experience inside the colors of the rainbow will be meaningful for you in a very special way.

As you relax in your comfortable chair, imagine an early morning rainfall. Listen to the rain as it gently taps on a window. The sound is lulling and soothing, comforting and relaxing. As the steady rhythm of the rain continues, you feel peaceful and quiet within yourself. Just enjoy this feeling for a while.

The raindrops begin to patter slowly now as the rain softly comes to an end. Looking outside, you see the sun beginning to emerge from behind white misty clouds that float leisurely through the sky. Opening the window, you feel the pleasant warmth of the summer day and you decide to go outside to enjoy the warmth and light of the sun.

As you step outside, everything looks bright and beautiful. You breathe in the freshness of the gentle breeze and experience the wonderful feeling of a rain shower that has just ended. Looking up at the sky, you notice the most beautiful rainbow you've ever seen. It inspires a feeling of awe and wonder inside you. The colors are vibrant and pure—a shimmering spectrum of colors blending into one another, vibrating perfectly in tune with each other.

As you're admiring the beauty of the rainbow, you sense the harmony of the colors and you decide to take a magical trip through the rainbow to experience and absorb the colors within your body and your mind. You want to feel what the colors are really like, to be inside the colors and in tune with the colors, understanding the unique energies and vibrations of each color.

Somehow you know that all you have to do is just relax into the rainbow and feel yourself flowing upward through the colors. As you enter the color red at the bottom of the rainbow, you begin to gradually blend into the color, breathing the color inside you and absorbing it within your body and your mind. You feel the color of red all around you as you flow through it and it flows through you and draws an image inside your mind. As you experience the color with every part of your awareness, you become part of the color. Your body and your mind and all your senses move in perfect rhythm and harmony with the color. As you absorb the color completely within yourself, you feel what the color is really like as you explore and understand the energies that vibrate to the color of red.

Rising into the color orange, you gradually blend into the color, breathing the color inside you, absorbing it within your body and your mind. Moving upward in a gentle motion, you feel the color of orange all around you as it flows through you and draws an image inside your mind. As you experience the color with every part of your awareness, you become part of the color, flowing through it as it flows through you. Your body and your mind and all your senses move in perfect rhythm and harmony with the color. Absorbing the color completely within yourself, you feel what the color is really like as you explore and understand the energies that vibrate to the color of orange.

Rising even higher into the rainbow, into the color yellow, your awareness blends easily, naturally, into the color as you breathe it inside you, absorbing it within your body and your mind. You feel the color of yellow all around you as it flows through you and draws an image inside your mind. As you flow through the color and experience it with every part of your awareness, you become part of the color. Your body and your mind and all your senses move in perfect rhythm and harmony with the color. Absorbing the color completely within yourself, you feel what the color is really like as you explore and understand the energies that vibrate to the color of yellow.

Flowing into the color green inside the rainbow, you blend easily into the color, breathing it inside you, absorbing it within your body and your mind. You feel the color green all around you as you flow through it and it flows through you and draws an image inside your mind. As you experience the color and the image it draws with every part of your awareness, you become part of the color. Your body, your mind, and all your senses move in perfect rhythm and harmony with the color. As you absorb the color completely within yourself, you feel what the color is really like as you explore and understand the energies that vibrate to the color of green.

Floating and rising higher inside the rainbow, into the color blue, you blend smoothly into the color, flowing through it and breathing it inside you, absorbing it within your body and your mind. You feel and sense the color of blue all around you and within you as it flows through you and draws an image inside your mind. As you experience the color with every part of your awareness, you become part of the color. Your body, your mind, and all your senses move in perfect rhythm and harmony with the color. Absorbing the color completely within yourself, you feel what the color is really like as you explore and understand the energies that vibrate to the color of blue.

Entering the color indigo, feeling it gradually surround you as you flow through it, you breathe it inside you, absorbing it within your body and your mind. You feel and sense the color of indigo all around you and within you as it flows through you and draws an image inside your mind. As you experience the color and the image with every part of your awareness, you become part of the color. Your body, your mind, and all your senses move in perfect rhythm and harmony with the color. Absorbing the color completely within yourself, you feel what the color is really like as you explore and understand the energies that vibrate to the color of indigo.

You're rising higher and higher inside the rainbow, into the color violet. Feeling it surround you, you breathe it inside you as you flow through it, absorbing it within your body and your mind. You feel and sense the color of violet all around you and within you as it flows through you and draws an image inside your mind. Experiencing the color with every part of your awareness, you become part of the color. Your body, your mind, and all your senses move in perfect rhythm and harmony with the color. Absorbing it completely within yourself, you feel what the color is really like as you explore and understand the energies that vibrate to the color of violet.

Reaching the top of the rainbow, you look above yourself and see a shimmering white mist. It sparkles with the essence of universal awareness and light, inviting you within. As you enter this shimmering white mist, it feels soft and warm, safe and secure, filled with joy and pure knowledge. You sense how special this light is. Gathering it all around you and breathing it inside you, you become part of the light, absorbing it within your body and your mind.

Reentering the rainbow, you flow softly and easily into the color violet, seeing your inner images again and remembering your feelings inside each color as you descend gradually and gently through all the colors you've experienced, flowing into indigo, blue, green, yellow, orange, and red.

Standing on the ground now, you look up at the rainbow that's blending into the sky and becoming part of the brilliant sunlight. In another moment, the rainbow seemingly disappears as it becomes part of the sky and the sunshine. You can no longer see it but you know it's still there, waiting for the appropriate time to become visible again.

While everything you experienced is clear in your mind, write down what you saw and felt inside each color. Completely describe the images you saw in your mind and define what they represent to you on an inner, feeling level. If the images were blurry or if you sensed them more than you saw them, that's OK. Be clear and detailed in your descriptions of what you experienced. You've just said "hi" to your subconscious and it responded by showing you images of your thoughts, feelings, and inner knowledge.

Visualization is the ability to see objects, scenes, and images inside your mind with your eyes closed. You see with your mind's eye, which is sometimes referred to as your *third eye* or your *mystic eye*. This is a natural ability, but if you have trouble seeing with your mind's eye at first, try this: Look at a picture or object of whatever you want to visualize. Concentrate your full attention on it. Notice all the details. Then close your eyes and re-create a picture of it in your mind or remember what it looks like. With a little bit of time and practice, you'll soon reactivate your inner sense of seeing. And keep this in mind: You already know how to visualize. You do it every night when you see images in your dreams.

It's just as important to open up and develop your inner sense of feeling—to sense what something feels like or to sense what it looks like. This helps you learn to listen to yourself—to read both your conscious and subconscious feelings, and to trust the knowledge you have within you. It helps you open up your intuition and the awareness of your inner self.

While the image or object that appeared in your mind can have a literal meaning, most often it shows you something symbolic on a feeling level that you associate with that particular color, with its vibration of energy. The meaning may be very spiritual and indicative of your inner knowledge or it may be a message that your subconscious mind is trying to tell you about on a conscious level. Remember that your subconscious talks to you through images and feelings, through pictures instead of words.

To understand the symbology of the image or object that you visualized and what it means and/or represents to you, ask your subconscious for the answer and let the thought come into your conscious mind. Ponder it a bit. Just let it be gentle on your mind. You'll begin to open up your inner awareness even more and to better understand what your subconscious is saying to you. Also, by doing Mind-Power Exercise #4 at the end of this chapter, you'll gain a clearer understanding of what your subconscious has shown you.

What you experienced in the energies of the rainbow are what the colors feel like to you. Each color has a different vibrational rate of energy. (Your favorite color shows what level of energy you feel most in tune with.) The vibrations of each color can be used to focus and direct the power of your mind on both a physical and a spiritual level. You can use the energies of a color to help you achieve specific purposes or to change the expressions of your experiences. By wearing clothes of a certain color or by imagining yourself to be surrounded by the color, you set the energies of that color into motion.

A general guide to the properties and qualities of each
color are described in the next few paragraphs, although
the intensity and hue of each color varies greatly and can
affect your attitude and emotions in very different ways.
For example, a neon green won't have the same effect as
a natural green. Also, the way you feel about a color will
help to determine how you respond to its energy.

Red increases your physical energy. Orange expands
your basic instincts. Yellow enhances your inner knowledge and helps you open up your intuitive nature and the
magical power of your mind. Green promotes healing and
harmony. Blue relaxes, calms, and soothes you. Indigo
opens up your psychic perceptions and enhances the mystical power of your mind. Violet helps you become more
aware of your true spiritual nature. The white light above
the rainbow is a universal energy that is very special and
powerful. Its many magical and mystical uses and applications will be covered throughout this book.

You can use the vibrations of the colors for many beneficial purposes. For example, the color blue. One of my
students, when faced with a stressful feeling or experience,
would imagine that he was putting it inside a blue envelope. Surrounding a feeling with the color blue takes the
edge off and calms it while preventing the energy of the
emotion from being focused and directed, either within or
outside yourself. He'd seal the envelope and let the emotion simmer down. When he was feeling calmer, he'd open

the envelope and take care of the negative emotion or experience in a peaceful, positive manner.

Another student, when she was involved in a negative experience, would take a deep breath and visualize jumping into the blue sky and sitting there for a while—getting a bigger, better view, a new perspective, an overall picture—until she felt like coming back down to earth and dealing with the situation.

If you feel sick, wear clothes that have green in them or close your eyes and envision yourself surrounded with the color of green. Or imagine yourself inside a garden that's very vibrant and alive with energy, with lots of lush, green plants and lots of bright, warm sunlight. This sets the healing energies of the color into motion and actually does make you feel better.

If you're feeling tired or have the blahs, wear something red or very colorful, or imagine splashes of bright color zipping through your mind. Just thinking about the color red can get your physical energies into high gear.

If you want to enhance your inner knowledge, imagine yourself surrounded with sunshine. Better yet, go outside and sit in the sun. Soak up the rays. Absorb the light into your body and your mind. Let your thoughts flow, free and easy; listen to them and watch the images they draw.

The possibilities are endless because your mind is limitless.

MIND-POWER EXERCISES

1. Relax several times a day and before you go to sleep at night. Get good at it, so that by just closing your eyes and taking a few deep breaths, your physical body completely relaxes and your conscious mind becomes calm and quiet. Really notice how you feel when you're relaxed. Note any thoughts or ideas that come to you when you're in this level of increased subconscious awareness.

2. Rise through the rainbow and reexplore the energies of the colors, including the white light above the rainbow. This enhances your awareness of energy vibrations and will help you develop the mystical power of your mind.

3. According to how you feel in each color of the rainbow, allow the vibrations of the color to help you in a beneficial way. You can experience whatever you imagine. Stretch your mind and see where it goes. Your subconscious mind already knows how to focus the energies of each color in a positive way. Follow your feelings and go with the flow of your thoughts.

4. Clearly visualize the images or objects you've seen inside each color of the rainbow. You may want to begin a journal that you can refer to from time to time, or you may prefer to just let your images and experiences flow through your mind. Either way is fine; do what feels right for you.

Write down or remember a very detailed description of the image or object. Include everything about it. Describe it so well that a blind person could virtually see it. This will help you increase your ability to visualize, to see with your mind's eye.

Get involved with your imagination to feel or sense what the images or objects are really like and what they represent to you. Go inside each one and see what your subconscious symbology is saying to you. Tune into the images' or objects' vibrational level of energy. This helps you understand the language of your mind and will also help you open up your imagination and develop your inner sense of feeling.

CHAPTER TWO

You and Your Self-Image

You're a unique, wonderful, magical person, inside and out. You're physical and spiritual at the same time. The only thing that you're not is perfect. But that's OK—neither am I. We all have our little quirks and eccentricities that make us special. And dare I say it? We all have a few little flaws, but I like mine. I accept them because they're part of me and because I know I can change them at any time. For the moment, they serve a useful purpose. Otherwise it would be silly to hang on to something that's no longer meaningful, something that couldn't help me see or learn more about myself, or something that couldn't help me grow in some way.

The way you see yourself can prove to be very interesting and enlightening. Your perceptions about yourself determine your self-image. The way you feel and think and act is reflected in your day-to-day thoughts and activities. Your self-image is formed by *your* belief of who you are. It's a mirror of your previous thoughts, feelings, beliefs, and actions, and is constantly in a process of change from the inside out. By taking an honest look at yourself and seeing everything there is to see, you can better understand your true feelings and become more aware of who you really are on the inside.

Your self-image isn't just the reflection you see looking back at you from the mirror every day. There's much more to you than that. The outer you is an expression of the inner and more real part of you. Your self-image includes everything about you—all your actions and interactions with the people and situations in your life, and all your thoughts and feelings, whether they're good or bad, ugly or beautiful. They're all part of you. They're part of what you've done, what you're doing now and what you'd like to do. You're part of the past, present, and future, all framed in a picture of now.

The total picture of you has also been shaped, in part, by other people's opinions and feelings about you. It's been influenced by friends, family, teachers, coworkers, and everyone you've ever known. Regardless of what other people think about you, however, your self-image has been formed and created entirely by *you* through *your* beliefs about yourself. Because you're responsible for you. You're responsible for either accepting or rejecting other people's opinions.

It's time to meet the real you. Think about how you see and feel about yourself, both on the outside and on the inside. The actions of the outer you mirror the thoughts and feelings of the inner you. In addition to all the wonderful things about yourself, think about the not-so-nice things, too. The things you're in the process of changing and the things you know that need some work—things you'd like to change. Before you can change anything about yourself, you have to acknowledge and accept who you are right now. By seeing things as they are, you give yourself the power to change and create anything you want.

If you want to change something about your self-image—about the way you see and feel about yourself or the way you act about something or react to someone— simply change your thoughts and feelings. Change your perceptions. Think about who you want to become. That's part of who you already are and will show you who you're in the process of becoming. Take a look and see.

Close your eyes and imagine a magical mirror in your mind. This mirror lets you look clearly within yourself to see, change, create, and become/be the perfect you—the ideal image of yourself the way you want to be. This magical mirror shows you the real you.

Look into this magical mirror and see yourself as you are now. As you're looking at your reflection, think about and appreciate all the positive inner qualities you possess. Now see yourself as your ideal image—who you want to be. See yourself with all the qualities you want to possess.

Keep in mind that you already possess them inside—otherwise you wouldn't be able to see them. Your ideal image is a true reflection of who you already are on the inside. Superimpose the images upon themselves and blend them together so that they become one. Say or think silently to yourself, "I've become who I am."

Next, put your ideal self-image into action through your belief of who you really are on the inside. See your image reflected in every part of your life—in your actions, your experiences, your relationships, and, most important, in your thoughts and feelings. Believe that you become more like your ideal image every day. This may take some time to occur, depending on what you believe about yourself. What you see on an inner level takes time to manifest on an outer level. However, your ideal self-image—the inner picture—is the real and true image.

Every time you look within yourself in this magical mirror, or you see yourself reflected through your thoughts, feelings, and actions in your day-to-day activities, see yourself through the eyes of your ideal image. Every time you think about your feelings and the qualities you're working on changing or bringing out in a clear and beautiful way, know that you already are that person. Every time you see yourself reflected in or through another person's feelings, actions, compliments, or even their complaints or criticisms, recognize that this is helping you become more perfect every day, in every way.

If your ideal image looks or acts differently than your self-image, that's OK. Continue to hold the picture of your ideal image in your mind. Then watch your self-image change and become your ideal image. It'll happen in the way that you believe it will happen. You're the one with the power to make it happen.

This magical mirror serves many wonderful purposes. It works by your imagination and belief. Since you already know that the possibilities are endless because your mind is limitless, you can use it right now in every part of your life to help you see, create, or change anything you want. Just use your imagination. It's more real than you think!

MIND-POWER EXERCISES

1. Finish this sentence: "I like myself because . . . " Write down one hundred or more reasons why you like yourself. List all your good qualities and features. Also include things such as big goals you've accomplished and little things you've done. You won't get conceited from doing this, unless you already have an oversized ego, but you will appreciate yourself more.

2. Think about the thoughtws and feelings that you'd like to change about yourself. This will show you who you're in the process of becoming and will show you the power you have within yourself to bring about inner changes that will soon begin to appear in your life.

3. Smile at yourself in the mirror. Note your feelings while you're doing this and write down why you feel the way you do. This will help you understand yourself better, and you might even see a magical thing or two that wasn't there before.

4. Take time every day to see the real you reflected in every part of your life and to appreciate how special you really are.

CHAPTER THREE

The Power of Words, Thoughts, and Feelings

Opening up the magical power of your mind and developing your mystical abilities occurs naturally as you build a foundation that is structured and framed by positive thoughts. A positive attitude is the first and most important part of building a strong and solid foundation, and it lays the necessary groundwork for opening up the power of your mind.

Your words and thoughts originate from your feelings. Feelings are more powerful than words or thoughts because feelings begin in your subconscious and inspire your words and thoughts. Your words, thoughts, and feelings set the stage for the way you experience everything in your life; they determine how you act and react in every situation.

Your attitude is based on what you think and how you feel and by what you say and do. If you want to develop a more positive attitude, it's a good idea to use positive words! Words are more than meaningless mumbles that fall out of your mouth. Watch what you say.

Your subconscious mind will do whatever you tell it to do. Suppose you have to give a speech or a business presentation. If you think to yourself, "Wow, I'm really nervous. I know I'm going to make a fool of myself, and I'll probably forget everything I want to say," your subconscious will help you make a fool of yourself and will ensure that you forget everything you want to say. Your body will cooperate by giving you sweaty palms, a dry mouth, rapid heartbeat, and the shakes.

By changing a few words, you can turn this into a positive experience and change the outcome. You can say, "I'm confident. I'm going to do great, and I'll remember everything I want to say." These words help to change your feelings and attitude, and all you've done is to substitute the opposite of the negative words to come up with a positive statement that your subconscious will respond to.

Take another look at that positive sentence, though. It's nice and it's a super step in the right direction, but it still sounds a little lame, doesn't it? There's no energy inside it, no vim and vigor and absolute surety. It's just positive words, maybe said doubtfully with dread and fear inside. Look at how much energy was invested in the negative sentence to begin with. Put some positive power inside those words!

Substituting positive words for negative words is a great way to improve your attitude and to change situations. But there's a catch. When you change the words, you have to change your feelings, too. Otherwise, you've changed the words and nothing else. You have to believe that your positive statement is true and that it reflects your real feelings, because your subconscious reads and interprets your feelings before it listens to and acts on your words.

Your subconscious mind responds to the words you use by acting on the mental pictures it draws from your words. Your subconscious acts upon the words that draw the most vivid images. And you should see what it does with your feelings.

Suppose you have a few extra pounds hanging around on your body, and you decide you'd like to lose some weight because you'd like to look and feel better. So you say to yourself, "I don't want to be fat." Looks like, sounds like, and seems like a positive sentence, but it's really a negative statement, because your subconscious only hears the word *fat* and acts upon that word. It draws a fat picture of you in your mind. Change the word *fat* to *slender* so that your sentence says, "I want to be slender." You have a positive statement and your subconscious responds to and acts upon the word *slender*.

But don't expect skinny right away. Before you become slender, you have some serious work to do. Part of it is probably physical exercise, but most of it is mental exercise. You have to change your thoughts and feelings, too, not just the word. Look at the thought and feelings that originated the words, "I don't want to be fat." How does your mind read that?

Your subconscious doesn't use complete sentences. It's not formal; it's friendly and it likes phrases. Your subconscious reads your feelings that say "extra pounds" (this guarantees you'll get even fatter), "hanging around body" (this ensures flab), and "lose some weight" (your subconscious refuses to lose anything because it's the storehouse of all your thoughts, memories, and knowledge and is the seat of your soul—and *weight* is a heavy word). There is one positive thought in there—"look and feel better"— but it's been neutralized because you *feel* that you look bad.

Take a good look at your vocabulary to see whether it's negative or positive. Some negatives are easy to recognize; others are less obvious. For example, "I won't get sick." Change to "I'm healthy." Notice the images that your mind draws and how much better you feel now. "I won't forget that." Change to "I'll remember." Your memory is improving already.

Negative contractions such as *can't* or *won't* place limits on you. Suppose you're in a situation you don't like. If you say, "I can't think of any way to get myself out of this situation," you're setting yourself up to remain in that situation, and you're blocking all positive avenues of escape because you used the words *I can't*. What else is wrong with that sentence? Pick it apart; look inside the thoughts and feelings.

Change the sentence to "I can think of lots of positive ways to get myself out of this situation." You've begun to change your attitude, but note your feelings—they're still negative. (Just wanted to see if you were paying attention!) And what does the word *escape* imply? Even though that word isn't in your sentence, the *feeling* of it is.

With the use of positive words, you can change your feelings about the situation and allow your mind to provide you with creative ways to get out of the situation you've placed yourself in. You might want to begin by throwing in a thought that goes something like this: "I got myself into this situation and I can get myself out of it." This shows your subconscious that you're accepting responsibility for the situation you've created. It shows that you're changing your feelings and you're willing to work toward a positive outcome. But there's still something negative in the sentence. What is it? Hint: the words "get myself out of." Change the words and see how you feel.

A good way to change the sentence, and the situation, is to say, "I can think of lots of positive ways to benefit from this situation." Maybe you can't, but say the words anyway. The words will begin to change the flow of energy and will open up thoughts and ideas that will help you see many positive ways to benefit from the situation. By using these words, you're doing more than just getting yourself out of the situation; you're turning it into something that you can enjoy and benefit from. And the situation itself will begin to change to provide you with insights and a new direction to go in.

Look into how you approach taking care of a situation. Suppose you're concerned about something and you think to yourself, "I'm **not going to worry** about it!" Your subconscious hears the word *worry* and that's exactly what you do. And notice that you stress the words, **not going to.** This adds power to your negative sentence because of your strong thoughts and feelings that originated from whatever it is that you're worried about.

So you say, "I'm not going to think about it." I guarantee you it will constantly be on your mind. The words *going to* are action words and you're *going to* do exactly what you told yourself you weren't going to do. Change this sentence for yourself. How would you turn "I'm not going to think about it" into a positive sentence/situation that reflects your positive feelings?

Sometimes, without consciously realizing it, you set up situations that appear to be positive, and then, by your words and feelings, you turn them into negative experiences. If you offer yourself several alternatives, just in case a situation doesn't work out the way you hope it will, you could be setting yourself up to fail. Your feelings that originated the alternatives reinforce doubts you hold and believe on a subconscious level. Maybe you're not aware of them so they fall into the murky realm of *un*conscious, which means *un*aware. On the other hand, you could be enhancing the situation and setting up some wonderfully creative and positive experiences, options, and alternatives. It depends on your perspectives and perceptions—the way you look at the situations you're involved in and how you feel about them.

You don't *have* to change anything about a situation unless you want to. Maybe you'd like to wait and see what happens as your situation unfolds—to gather information and ideas and answers about it, to become aware of certain things you might need to see so you can move forward—and to see how you really feel about it. It can be very positive to sit back, relax, and go with the flow—to enjoy your situation by seeing all the positive parts of it and how it opens up, and by allowing it to be a wonderful learning experience that leads you in the direction you want to go.

Some negative situations are complex and complicated but can become powerful and positive through your perceptions and attitude. Suppose you don't like your boss at work. It's important to be realistic and honest about your feelings—to see things as they are and acknowledge that you don't like your boss. If you say, "My boss *really* bothers me," you're making a negative statement. You rephrase your sentence by changing the words to "My boss doesn't bother me." All you're doing is rearranging words and reinforcing a negative thought, even though you've phrased it in a milder tone. You're still allowing your boss to bother you (plus this stupid sentence is probably getting on your nerves and you're getting aggravated because now you're thinking about your boss!).

There are lots of ways you can change the words and the situation so that your words reflect a positive statement. How about "My boss provides me with a wonderful opportunity to learn more about myself," or "Working for my boss shows me that I can do things in a better and more efficient way," or "My boss has provided me with the incentive to look for and to find a much better job." Sounds good, and it's a super start. Look underneath these positive sentences to see if the fact that your boss bothers you is still lurking there, or if you've truly changed your perceptions.

It's imperative that your feelings match the words you use. Underneath the words, your feelings assess what the words mean to you. Then your feelings direct your actions, regardless of your words. If your feelings don't match the words you use, you're making a negative statement no matter what you say because your feelings win out over your words.

However, with your positive words your attitude toward your boss *does* begin to change, maybe ever so slightly at first, because you're phrasing your words in a positive way and this is a very powerful step toward changing your feelings. As soon as you begin to believe in and act on your positive words, your boss loses all the power you've previously given him or her to bother you. You've reclaimed your power and now you're using it to help yourself.

When your feelings support your positive statements, you can change this negative situation into a positive one. By accepting responsibility for your situation, your self-esteem and self-worth soar. You're looking for and finding the good in the situation. In addition, you're aware of your power to change it and you're inspiring yourself to take positive action. More importantly, your feelings about yourself change to reflect your positive attitude and you empower yourself, rather than giving your power away.

Some of the less obvious negatives in your vocabulary are words framed with negative feelings. For example, the word *should* is negative. If you feel that you *should* do something, then it's something you don't want to do but for some reason feel you have to do or you feel obligated to do it. Or even worse, someone told you to do it, and they said it in a controlling or a threatening way. When you use the words *I want to* or *I'd like to* instead of the word *should*, it changes your feelings and your attitude, and you look forward to doing something that you *want* and *like* to do rather than doing something you feel you *should* do.

Some negative words are a bit tricky to recognize because they're disguised as positive words. *Hope* is a negative word. When you use the word *hope*, you may think you're making a positive statement, such as, "I hope

I'll be able to achieve this." The words *able to achieve* are positive but aren't quite up to par for a super-positive person. Their power was destroyed when you prefaced them with *hope*.

Your feelings interpret the word *hope* as negative because your feelings are that you may or may not be able to achieve what you want. You're only hoping that it's possible. You're acknowledging and accepting doubt, and you're giving your power away. Change the word *hope* to *believe* and see how your feelings change. When you *believe* you'll be able to achieve what you want, you're well on your way to success. Better yet, change the word *believe* to the word *know* and the words *able to* to the word *can* so that your statement says, "I *know* I *can* achieve this."

This is a really powerful sentence, but you're keeping yourself stuck with those words even though they're positive. You didn't give the words or yourself any place to go. You and your words are just sitting there quivering with anticipation and energy, waiting for a direction to move into so the words can spring into action and you can achieve whatever it is that you want to achieve.

Back up your words with actions. "Actions speak louder than words." It's an old axiom, but it's very true. One of my students once said to me, "It's better to act a new way of thinking than to think a new way of acting." Wise words. When you put action into your words and thoughts, watch what happens. The first thing you'll see is that your mind will open up with lots of creative ideas and pictures that will show you how to achieve what you want.

Recognize the negatives before they sneak into your subconscious and do their dirty work. Change them into positives that put the power of your thoughts and feelings into your words. Positive energy behind a positive thought always brings a positive result. Your attitude toward everything in your life will determine your response to and the outcome of any situation you're in. As you change your words, thoughts, and feelings and you become more positive and powerful, it's very important to move toward what you want, rather than away from what you don't want. These words appear to say the same thing, but they make a world of difference in how you direct your energies.

Changing negatives into positives can be a challenging experience at times. You may find yourself in some situations that appear to be unchangeable, even though you've changed your words, thoughts, and feelings. What you *can* do is change your perspective and perception of the situation. Look at it differently. This opens up ideas and insights, and changes your feelings even further, which will change your attitude and your response, and then somehow—as if by some mysterious magic or quirk of fate—the situation itself will change, or solutions you'd never dreamed of before will pop into your mind.

For every negative situation you're in that appears to be unchangeable, begin by looking at it as a challenge rather than a problem. If you look at your situation as a problem, then a problem—with all of its negative implications—exists. When you look at something as a challenge, it becomes something positive and you look forward to working with it. By using your situation as a springboard to create new, positive circumstances, your mind will automatically respond in a creative and positive way.

Make sure you feel good about the words you use. Pay attention to the images and feelings they inspire inside you. I love the word *challenge* because it fills me with energy and inspires me into positive action. I rise up to challenges. They bring to mind images of being the master of my fate and visions of changing and creating a new and better situation, world, environment, relationship, or whatever.

But some people feel uncomfortable with the word *challenge*. They much prefer the word *opportunity*. That brings to my mind gentle, quiet—yet equally powerful—changes. Through your own positive words, thoughts, and feelings, you can either give yourself a wonderful opportunity or an exciting challenge. And your first challenge or opportunity can be that of relearning and rewriting your vocabulary in a positive way.

Your positive words, thoughts, and feelings will open the magical power of your mind. Here's a homework assignment for you. Make a list of negative words you've previously used. Change the words to positive words. Make sure your feelings correspond with the words you use. Pay attention to what you *aren't* saying as well as to what you *are* saying. For each word, write down what the negative word implies and what the meaning of the positive word is.

I'll do the first one for you. *Negative words*: homework assignment. *Negative implication*: homework is something I *should* do that I don't want to do. It's too much work and no fun, and it interferes with my social life. Plus, I don't have time and my pencil broke. I'll tell the teacher that my dog ate my papers, but I doubt she still believes that one. *Positive words*: Mind-Power Exercise. *Positive meaning*: oh, wow!! Mind-Power Exercise sounds like something really fun and interesting to do that offers me a great way to see some very powerful things within myself. I can help myself to become more aware of everything and to be more positive in every part of my life. I'm going to do the exercises right now. Where's that pencil sharpener? Oh, yeah. The dog will probably be happier too because now he can eat real food instead of scraps of crumpled-up paper.

Get the idea? Now do a few or more on your own and see what you come up with. Choose real-life examples, words that you use. By the way, I've heard some very creative excuses from my students when they didn't do their homework. Excuses are negative. Get your mind into motion and exercise those positive muscles. The benefits are wonderful and can be life changing.

MIND-POWER EXERCISES

1. Some of the following sentences are obviously negative. Others may appear to be positive, but look below the surface. Put yourself inside these sentences, as if you'd said or thought them. Change them into positive sentences that reflect your feelings. After you've changed them, look at what they really say. If they're still negative, change them again and also change your feelings.

1. I'm so bored. I don't have anything interesting to do and there's no one here to talk to.
2. Nothing ever works for me and no one likes me.
3. I'll never get this job. I know they didn't like me, and they probably thought I wasn't qualified.
4. Today looks like it's going to be as bad as yesterday was, maybe even worse.
5. I'm not going to let anyone talk me into doing something I don't want to do.
6. I don't feel like making dinner tonight. It's too much trouble.
7. I can't get everything done. I don't have enough time.
8. I really hate my boss at work. He's an idiot.
9. I should make an appointment to go to the dentist.
10. I refuse to get upset when my kid/friend/spouse/whoever bothers me.

11. I can't believe I spent that much money on a new sweater.
12. I feel sorry for that kid down the street who broke his leg. Now his whole summer is ruined.
13. I wish I hadn't quit my job.
14. I've got to start that new diet soon. I'll have to exercise, too, if I'm ever going to lose weight.
15. I'm always going to be nice to everyone.
16. I should apologize to my brother for telling him to leave me alone. I guess I was a little nasty to him, but he keeps telling me about his problems and begging me for money.
17. I hate going grocery shopping on Saturdays, but it's the only time I can go. The store is too crowded and someone always runs into me with their cart.
18. Instead of cleaning the house today, I'm going to call my friends.
19. None of my friends is home. They're probably all at the grocery store. What a rotten day! Now I've got the blahs. Maybe I'll try to relax. Didn't work; guess I'm too tense. I'm just going to sit here and watch TV. Nothing is on except stupid cartoons. Maybe I'll do my Mind-Power Exercises. But there's so many of them. Maybe I'd better not do them in this frame of mind.
20. I've decided to be a more positive person.

2. Imagine that the following scenarios are really happening to you. How would you react to these situations
and what would you do? For each scenario, write down
your immediate reaction and response. Be honest about
how you'd feel and what you'd think about doing. Look
at your feelings and the plan of action you'd pursue.

Then give the same situation a more careful, considered,
positive treatment. Write down how you'd change the situation and turn it into a positive experience. Notice the
difference, if any, between your first reaction and second
look at the same situation. Notice if and how your perspectives and perceptions changed.

- Scenario #1: Oh God, it's Monday. You wake up
  with a headache. The fight you had last night with
  your best friend/kid/spouse/whomever is still on your
  mind. The aspirin bottle is empty. The shower isn't
  working; there's no hot water. There's nothing for
  breakfast—not even a cup of coffee—because you
  didn't go grocery shopping on Saturday.

  You go out to your car. It's thundering, lightning,
  and pouring rain. Your car won't start; the battery
  is dead because you left the lights on all night. You
  go back into the house to call your office to say
  you'll be late. This is the fifth time this month that
  you're late for work and they've threatened to fire
  you if you're late again. The phone isn't working.

  You're becoming more than a little upset. You
  go over to the neighbors' house to use their phone to

call the office and the motor club. None of your neighbors are home, and there's no one to help you. It's raining harder than before. You realize that you've left your keys in the house, so now you can't get back in.

- SCENARIO #2: You lost your job three months ago. You've been on sixty-three interviews and no one wants to hire you for reasons that you think are dumb. You've used up every cent of your savings and your landlord/mortgage holder is threatening eviction/foreclosure.

- SCENARIO #3: You receive a letter from the IRS informing you that you're going to be audited. You wonder how they found out you cheated on your taxes, when you thought you'd covered your tracks so well.

3. Look at the negative situations in your life that you're currently involved with in a more positive light. Become aware of how your thoughts, feelings, words, and previous actions created the current situation. Write down the situation as it exists now and list all the positive things about it. Prepare a plan of action in your mind and pursue it. Put your positive thoughts and feelings into action and watch the positive things that begin to happen with your current situation.

4. Think and act like a positive person because you *are* a positive person!

CHAPTER FOUR

Neutralizing the Negatives

The power of suggestion is very potent, but it's not always positive. Sometimes negativity can creep into your subconscious mind unaware. Clearing both your conscious and subconscious minds of negativity allows you to be completely in charge of your life. By recognizing negative situations and suggestions—by seeing what's really being said and done—you can change the way you unconsciously react to things.

Subconsciously you're aware of everything. Your subconscious doesn't miss a thing. Negative suggestions come in many forms and disguises, and can slip into your subconscious without your conscious awareness and permission if you're not paying close attention. Every day you hear imperceptible messages that bypass your conscious mind and enter your subconscious mind, which accepts and acts on what it hears. Your subconscious doesn't analyze or judge whether something is positive or negative; it simply accepts. Analyzing and judging are characteristics of your conscious mind.

By becoming aware of negative suggestions, learning how to read and recognize them on a conscious level, and either accepting or rejecting them, you can be in complete control of all your thoughts and feelings. Negative suggestions are like termites that get into your house and eat away at the foundation until your house crumbles; negative suggestions can do terrible things to your frame of mind and erode your positive attitude. But they're easy to recognize once you know what to look for. It's important to realize when these subtle, sometimes silent, and always sneaky negative suggestions try to enter your subconscious, because then you can stop them in their tracks and change them into positive suggestions that reflect your positive nature. Here are some things to look out for:

ADVERTISING. Although a few ads are informative and entertaining, it seems that most advertising tries to plant negative suggestions into your subconscious. You're attacked by ads that you hear every day on the radio and on TV and those that you read in magazines and newspapers. The ad usually starts with a personal put-down, asking you how you ever managed before they came along to save you, revs up with a statement that the advertiser can do something better than someone else or has a better product than their competitor, and ends by insulting your intelligence with a statement that you need this product and can't be happy or successful without it.

For example, I saw an offer for a magazine subscription that read, "If you have a bold and inquiring mind, this invitation is for you." This suckers you into subscribing to the magazine. It doesn't matter whether the magazine is something you're interested in. You're buying it to prove to yourself that you've got a bold and inquiring mind. The way to counteract this is to know that you already have a bold and inquiring mind and that you're much too smart to fall for their advertising campaign.

Television commercials seem to be specifically designed to hit you in a vulnerable spot or to make you feel guilty. Picture this: Cute baby, crying because his diaper leaks. Frown of concern on mother's face. Now the baby is wearing the advertiser's diaper, and he's happy and smiling. His mother is happy, too, because now she's a good mom. The spoken message between the tears and the smile is, "Caring moms buy our diaper." What's not spoken, but loudly implied, is a direct assault on your emotions: "You're a terrible mom and you don't care about your baby if you don't buy our diaper."

An ad in a New Age magazine for an expensive self-help workshop reads: "If your car was broken, you'd pay $300 to fix it. Isn't your mind worth at least as much as your car?" The unwritten message: "You're helpless, your life is a mess, and you don't know how to fix your mind. I'm the expert and I'm the only one who can help you. If you don't attend the workshop, it shows that you don't care about yourself." This attacks the very essence of your self-worth, among other things, and is perpetrated by someone who knows better than to play mind games. Shame on them!

Then there's the telemarketing call that always seems to come when you're extremely busy or eating dinner: "I'm calling for the policeman's association. Our boys work very hard to keep the streets safe, and sometimes they give their lives for you. Would you be kind enough to buy a raffle ticket for $25?" The message is designed to lay a guilt trip on you: If you don't buy the ticket, you're not a kind person, and even worse—you don't appreciate the cops or care that they're out there dying for you. When I received this call, I counteracted with, "I am a kind person and thank you for calling. Have a nice evening. Bye." I'm sure he thought my answer was strange but for the rest of the evening, I thought about the sincerely kind things people have done for me and I've done for them. I also thought about how the policemen chose their career and that they made the decision to risk their lives, if need be, and I respect the courage they have.

MUSIC. Most songs tell a woeful tale about sadness, despair, and unhappiness. Pay attention to the words in the song you're hearing. If you like the singer or the melody, you'll automatically accept the negativity in the words of the song.

Many people exercise to music. In addition to affecting you mentally and emotionally, music reacts with your muscular and nervous systems. Certain kinds of music have been proven to kill plants. Take a guess at what it can do to your physical and mental health. In addition to the words, music is sound and sound is energy. This energy, in the form of sound-wave vibrations, can either create harmony or wreak havoc on your body and your mind.

FRIENDS, FAMILY, AND COWORKERS. Negative suggestions aren't limited to music and advertising. They're everywhere, all the time. Every day, you're more or less battered and bombarded by negative statements from your friends, family, coworkers, and almost everyone else you meet. People often say things that are unintentionally negative, but appear to be positive and this sets you up for conflicting feelings. Most of the time you're not aware that their statements are negative, and you end up feeling terrible without knowing why.

For instance, one of your friends says to you, "You look tired today." You know that your friend has your best interests at heart and that she's concerned about you, but look closely at the statement and what it implies. It's easy to accept the negative because it's nice that your friend cares about you, but if you accept the statement, you will be tired. When you accept the positive—that your friend is concerned about you—you also accept and allow the negative suggestion to become effective.

You can counteract this with a stronger, more positive and powerful statement of your own. You can say, "I feel really great today." Even if you feel tired, your subconscious hears and responds to the positive statement that you feel great. What ultimately happens is that you begin to feel great because you've told yourself that you feel great. You've neutralized and counteracted the negative suggestion by replacing it with a stronger, more positive statement.

Suppose you tell someone about a project you're working on or an idea about something special you want to accomplish, and he or she says, "Yeah, you've said this before and nothing ever came of it. Besides, you'll never be able to accomplish it because it's too hard." That person is throwing failure in your face. If you say, "This project is different from the other one that I changed my mind about. It's not difficult and I *will* accomplish it," you haven't counteracted the negative suggestions that your subconscious will respond to because, although you've acknowledged that you changed your mind about the other project, you've also allowed self-doubt and defensiveness to creep into your words and feelings about your current project. You've reinforced and added negativity to the statements first made by someone else. The project you were so excited and happy about starts to look and feel like a lot of hard work and you begin to wonder if it's worth it, and you wish you hadn't said anything at all.

You can counteract and change negative suggestions like these and prevent them from getting into your subconscious, and ultimately your unconscious. One way to do this is to interrupt the person in midsentence. Never mind that you may seem rude. It's even more rude of them to say such negative things to you. What you're doing is affirming your power and preserving your positive attitude. Interrupt them with, "That other project served a very useful purpose. It showed me how to accomplish this one. I really know what I'm doing now and I've found the best way to do it. Besides, I've already completed it (or most of it), and it was easy and a lot of fun." Although you may not have accomplished it yet on a physical level, once you've thought of it and decided to do it, you have accomplished it on an inner level. The use of a positive past-tense statement reinforces your positive goal. But check out your feelings on this one. If you don't believe your statement is true, then it's worthless.

You could say, "I'm working on it and everything is going great." This sentence is fine for the moment, but it may not shut up your friend and it sounds defensive and leaves lots of room for negativity to set in later. To counteract this type of situation while it's occurring, be secure in what you're doing and have a firm belief in yourself. Smile at what your friend says. You know the truth. To

prevent this from happening, keep quiet or keep a low profile on whatever you're doing until after you've accomplished it or until it's strong enough to stand on its own.
Secrecy is very magical; it builds power and generates
energy toward your goal. If it's special, keep it secret. And
when it's done, share it with a big smile on your face!

BODY LANGUAGE. Negativity can be picked up through
other people's body language and facial expressions. Suppose someone frowns at you or looks at you in a disap-
proving way, e.g., with an arched eyebrow or a smirk. You
can react to this by smiling or you can give them a big,
friendly hug and tell them how much you like them. These
are really positive ways to cancel out and counteract this
type of negative. If it's gone past this point and you've
allowed that person to get to you, you can always resort
to a time-tested tactic that works wonderfully well. Make
faces at him or her behind his or her back. Although that's
childish, it's a lot of fun and it makes you laugh. And
laughter will return you to your positive attitude.

Here's something you run into every day: You see someone you know and ask how she is. She says, "I'm fine,"
but says it with a frown on her face and a slump to her
shoulders. Is she fine? I wouldn't think so, and after you
see her frown, you're not fine either.

Pay attention to the way people say words—to the way
their voice reflects their feelings by their intonation, inflec-
tion, and facial expression. People say so much more with

body language and tone of voice than just the words they use. Listen to the way the words are said. The words may be positive, but the feelings may not be.

PUSHY SALESPEOPLE. Negative suggestions can make you unhappy with something you're perfectly happy with. It's uncanny how salespeople home in on your weak spots. They work against your happiness and attempt to wear you down by planting strong seeds of doubt in your mind that usually attack you on a personal level. They put unrelated things into the picture that deceive you into thinking they're inextricably connected. They hit you where it hurts and try to make you feel stupid by pretending to know more than you do or by presuming to know you better than you know yourself.

For example, suppose your vacuum cleaner is old, but it does the job. (Did you catch the negativity in this sentence?) Along comes a vacuum cleaner salesman to your door with a brand-new model, saying that he was referred by your best friend. The salesman's vacuum cleaner looks better than yours, it has more features, and it's very expensive. He gives you his sales pitch, occasionally saying things like, "I'll bet you didn't know that," or suggesting that your life could be better, filled with parties and fun people, and that you'll have more friends and be happier if your rug is cleaner. He points out that you were sitting at home all alone with nothing better to do than clean your rugs before he came to the door.

You decide against buying his vacuum cleaner because, first, he's really irritating, and second, yours works fine and you're happy with it. After he leaves, you vacuum your rugs, and maybe you become a bit dissatisfied with your vacuum cleaner because you start thinking that the rug isn't as clean as it could be, and didn't he tell you that you'd have more friends if your rug was cleaner? You decide, what the heck, your rug is clean enough and so what if you had a fight with your best friend last week. It wasn't because you had dirty rugs, was it?

But now you're unhappy with your vacuum cleaner and with your life, too. In tears, you call the salesman and order his vacuum cleaner, all the time feeling bad about yourself and not knowing exactly why, hoping that by using his vacuum cleaner your life will improve and you'll make up with your best friend.

Be on guard for negative suggestions so you can cancel and counteract them. There are many ways to do this. The best way is to develop your own plan of action—one you feel good about that will work for you. This can be a lot of fun, and will show you how creative you can be when dealing with negative suggestions, situations, or people.

Returning to the vacuum-cleaner example: As soon as the salesman suggests that your rug is dirty, you could pull out your vacuum cleaner and say, "Yeah, I noticed that, too. There's a really dirty spot right where you're standing." Turn your vacuum cleaner on, wave the hose at him in a friendly yet somewhat threatening manner, and smile.

Then tell him to leave—you have better things to do than clean your rug.

Whatever you do, take care of the situation or suggestion right away by first being aware of the negative implications. Recognize what the message is saying, how your subconscious is interpreting it, and, most important, how you're reacting to it. Second, cancel the negative suggestions before they obtain a foothold. Do this immediately before they sink in and are accepted and absorbed by your subconscious and ultimately your unconscious. Third, do more than neutralize them. Make a stronger, more positive statement. Turn the negative suggestion inside out and around; reword it into a true reflection of your positive attitude. You're doing a lot more than neutralizing a negative; you're calling your complete awareness into action and using the magical power of your mind.

YOU. Now that you know what to look for, I'm sure you wouldn't ever intentionally give negative suggestions to anyone. But without being aware of it, you do it. It's an easy trap to fall into because on the surface many statements appear to be positive. And watch out for what you say to yourself. Sometimes we do the worst things to ourselves without consciously realizing what we're doing.

For example, you're on the phone with a friend setting up a tennis match. You compare schedules to find a convenient time for both of you. How often have you said, "Next week is bad for me—how about the week after?"

What you've done is to set up the entire next week to be bad for you. And you thought you were only making plans for a tennis match with your friend.

Look at what you do with "Oh God, it's Monday." That simple statement demolishes the start of the week, usually beginning over the weekend and lasting through midday Wednesday. By then you're seriously into the "Thank God, it's Friday" frame of mind. A positive ray of hope. You *are* going to get through this week after all. Not so. That statement destroys the remainder of the week. About 7:00 P.M. on Friday, after happy hour or whatever you do to adjust your attitude, you're finally relaxed and happy. This good feeling usually lasts about ten minutes before the thought hits you that Monday comes after the weekend.

Here's another example. One of your friends has just lost her job, and she's feeling bad about it. She probably overdid the "Oh God, Thank God" thing, and her boss fired her because he didn't like her attitude. She's worrying about money, dealing with rejection, and feeling fearful about finding a new job. You attempt to cheer her up and comfort her by saying, "I know it's rough, but you'll make it. You'll find another job." Then you tell her about when you lost your job, and how you almost starved to death and were evicted because you couldn't pay the rent, but eventually you found another job after sixty-three interviews and you know she will, too.

All of that is loaded with negativity. You're making your friend feel worse instead of better. You're making it even more difficult for her to deal with the rejection of being fired, and god knows what you're doing to her fear of how she's going to survive until she finds another job. All you wanted to do was to help; to give your friend positive encouragement, but you've really done the opposite, and that's not the worst of it. You're impeding her from allowing her experience to become an enjoyable time to explore new options, to grow and change, and you may be blocking her from seeing that now she has a wonderful opportunity to find or create a job she'll be happier with.

Suppose one of your friends—let's hope it's not the same one in the above example; you've done enough to her already—is sick. You sympathize by saying, "I know you feel crummy, but you'll get better. I remember when I had the flu. I was really sick for two weeks. I threw up every day, etc., so on and so forth, but I got better and so will you." Or you say, "I know you feel lousy so I'll bring over some chicken soup and maybe that will help you feel better."

It's nice that you care about your friend, but all you gave him were negative suggestions. You also neutralized your positive suggestions. There were two of them, but they were actually negative, i.e., chicken soup and "maybe that will help you feel better." No one eats chicken soup unless they're sick, so you were reinforcing the fact that he was sick. The words *feel better* are wonderful, but you prefaced them with *maybe* and connected them with the soup so the words *feel better* were neutralized and didn't register at all.

And look at what you did to yourself. By sympathizing with him, you're encouraging and allowing yourself to become sick. You're bringing up negative memories of when you were sick, and since you painted such a vivid, clear, graphic picture, your subconscious hears and responds to what you've said. So don't be surprised when you end up with the flu. It's not just the germs that get you.

Hopefully your friend is a very positive person and when you call him to tell him that *you're* sick, he says, "Wow! You have a few days to relax and do whatever you want to do. I read a great book last week. It's about the magical power of your mind. I'll bring it over for you. I know you'll really like it."

Your friend is offering you more than a book to read. He's offering you positive suggestions. He's acknowledging that you feel sick, which shows he cares about you, and he's helping you to see some positive ways of enjoying the time to yourself rather than offering sympathy and soup.

Look thoroughly into all the situations that you're involved with to see if they're negative or positive. Your feelings will tell you the truth and will offer you many creative ways to deal with anything and everything that comes into your life.

Since you're a more positive person now because you know how to recognize the negatives and neutralize them, and you can see the power of positives and formulate a positive plan of action that will work for you, here are a few feelings that you might want to consider changing:

1. SYMPATHY. Feeling sorry for someone can prevent him or her, as well as you, from realizing the positive potentials of the situation. See the Mind-Power Exercise about the kid with a broken leg in the previous chapter. It only looked as if his summer was ruined. His mom bought him a paint-by-number set. He enjoyed it so much that she bought him some tubes of paint and several blank canvasses and he learned how to paint. Today he's an artist who makes his living by painting.

2. REGRETS. *Could have been, if only,* etc. By entertaining regrets, you reinforce past failures instead of looking at them as positive learning experiences that contribute to success. Regrets hold you back from exploring and opening up new and very wonderful experiences. Let regrets be your springboard into positive action.

3. BLAME. Blame and complain are close cousins, and are related to resentment and hostility. It's easy to blame someone or something else when things go wrong or to com-

plain about a person or situation, but we create our own reality and we're responsible for everything we bring into our lives. Blaming and complaining keeps you stuck in the same place and prevents you from empowering yourself to change the situation or to let go of it.

4. ENVY. Envy and jealousy only make you feel helpless, because you don't realize that what you're envious or jealous of is something that you already have or have the ability to create but don't yet recognize. Let envy or jealousy show you what you can aspire to.

5. EMPATHY. When you empathize with someone's feelings or situation, you're feeling exactly the same emotions they are. Since feelings are very powerful, you'll accept the negative emotions that belong to someone else as your own. Whatever you're empathizing with will pull you down and place your energies on the same level. There are many ways to be supportive and show that you care without doing the drama.

6. ANGER. Anger and rage are very powerful, violent, and destructive emotions. Look into your anger to see what brought it forth. When you understand what triggers your anger, you know yourself better and can develop positive ways of dealing with your emotions and expressing what you're feeling. It's important to release your anger in constructive ways. If you keep it inside, it can do terrible things to you, from the inside out.

7. WORRY. Worries and anxieties set you into a *poor little me* frame of mind. This creates a sense of helplessness and keeps you locked in a never-ending cycle of negative emotions that go nowhere. *Poor little you* is powerless. By taking positive action, you can change that attitude.

8. GUILT. Guilt originates from both your misperceived expectations of yourself (beware the shoulds) and from other people's expectations of you. It occurs when you try to please everyone but yourself. With guilt as your companion, you're not able to look inside and see the positives. You're keeping yourself stuck to the negatives like glue. Let guilt become a good learning experience that inspires you. Turn it inside out so that it helps, rather than hinders, you.

You have the power to change all the negative emotions and experiences you encounter very simply and easily by applying one emotion that definitely belongs in your life— **happiness**. Being happy with yourself and with everything in your life will cancel, counteract, clear, and neutralize any and all negative situations and suggestions, whether the negativity comes from friends, family, advertising, or any other source.

Look for, find, and appreciate all the positives in your life. If they aren't obviously apparent, then they're hidden in the negatives or are on the opposite side of them. Enjoy all your experiences. They make life fun and interesting. No matter what happens to you or what anyone else says or does, the most powerful and magical thing you can do is to simply be happy. Create joy for yourself. And smile a lot. It makes people wonder what you've been up to.

MIND-POWER EXERCISES

1. Every day, list in your mind or write down at least seven positive things that:

- someone did for you,
- happened to you,
- you did for someone else, and
- you did for yourself.

This will help you see and recognize all the positives that you may not have previously paid attention to. Appreciate the little things as much as the large things. This can also turn a rotten day around and bring you up when you're feeling down. It's impossible to be sad when you're thinking about happy things.

2. Look at the negative situations you're experiencing now or suggestions that are influencing you. Note the origin of them, paying special attention to why you're feeling and reacting the way you are. Think about what you're

doing to neutralize the negativity and to replace it with positive suggestions and situations. Find as many positive items about the situation as you can. This will help you see inside the negatives and show you the power you have to turn them into positives.

If the situation involves another person, or if a person has given you negative suggestions, find as many positive things about the person as you can. This helps you see their good qualities and allows you to have positive feelings about that person.

3. Look at all the situations where you've either given or received positive suggestions. Note the situation, what the suggestion was, and how it made you feel. This helps you become more consciously aware of your thoughts and feelings, and the magical power you have to create happiness and joy in your life.

CHAPTER FIVE

Choices and Changes

You are a powerful, positive person. One of the most powerful things you can do in your life is to make choices and changes. You can turn any negative situation around into a positive experience. You have that power within you now. It isn't something that you have to learn; it's something you already know how to do.

Take problem solving, for instance. A problem can only exist in your life if you allow it to, if you direct negative thoughts and feelings toward the problem and energize it. When you change your perception—your thoughts and feelings—you change the focus and direction of your energy, thereby changing how you experience the problem. Problems are energy turned the wrong way. Turn them inside out and around, and you have a lot of energy to work with—to shape, form, and fashion in any way you choose. When you solve a problem, you're turning negative energy into positive energy.

A problem is really a positive learning experience in disguise. It provides a way for you to understand yourself better and offers you many wonderful opportunities. Look on the bright side of things. For every problem you create, you also create opportunities at the same time. Inside every problem, you'll find fabulous opportunities. They may be disguised or hidden, and sometimes they might be hard to recognize, but they're always there.

Recognizing opportunities is like finding the silver lining in a cloud. You have to look within the cloud to find it, just like looking within your mind for the solution to a problem. The cloud (problem) is a manifestation of negative thoughts that obscures the positive opportunities hidden within (silver lining/solution).

A problem is merely an outer appearance of your inner thoughts and feelings. When you change your thoughts and feelings, you change the way the problem shows itself. All you have to do to solve a problem is to change your perception of it and the problem disappears, much like a cloud disappears when the sun shines on it. As you look for the opportunities within your problems, you'll see that they provide a way for you to move forward in your life in a positive way. Some examples are:

- Being fired from a job: You have a wonderful opportunity to get a better job, to meet new and interesting people, to change careers, or to create your own job where you can do whatever you've always wanted to do. You have the freedom to do anything you choose.

- Getting divorced or having a relationship turn sour: This gives you a wonderful opportunity to look into yourself—into your feelings—to know yourself better and to grow emotionally.

REALITY CHECK: It's perfectly natural and normal to feel sad or depressed when you lose a friend or a lover. Give yourself time for you. Feel the hurt, pain, anger, or whatever emotions you're feeling to get unstuck from the negative aspects of a relationship. These emotions will help you get over the loss and see what you've gained. Give yourself permission to grow or to realize that you've outgrown that person.

When you think of him or her again after you've gotten past the pain, remember the good that you both shared, the good that you gave each other. Look at the many ways he or she helped you and you helped him or her. This allows you to go forward in your life with joy and happiness instead of sadness and despair. Celebrate the relationship you shared, rather than regretting it or feeling bitter.

- Not having something work out that you really wanted: This means that there's something better for you and gives you time to appreciate what you have, to review your choices, and to consider changes and new directions. This can open up your horizons tremendously and show you a new world right in front of you that perhaps you couldn't see before. It lets you regroup and change your mind, to energize other options and choices, and to explore different avenues.

Look at the so-called problems that you've experienced or are experiencing now to see the opportunities contained within. View the problems in a positive way to see why you've created them, what you want to learn from them, and what they have to offer you. You may surprise yourself with all the wonderful opportunities and choices you've given yourself to make positive changes. While you're doing that, you may also become aware that what you think of as a problem may not be a problem at all; it may only be a potential problem that you can prevent from occurring.

One of the best, and probably the most positive, ways to take care of a problem is to solve it *before* it actually becomes a problem. When you do this, you're working with an intangible—something that is not yet physically apparent. You're dealing with it on a *cause* level, where it's first created in your mind by your thoughts and feelings, before it becomes an *effect*—something tangible that occurs in your life.

It's easy to recognize potential problems. There are several early warning signs that precede the physical appearance of a problem. There's almost always an uneasy feeling, maybe vague, that *something* is wrong, something you can't quite put your finger on or put into words. You may have flashes of insight or see fleeting images of what might happen in the future. When you look into these feelings and images, you're using the magical power of your mind—your natural psychic abilities—to help you realize that a possible problem is brewing.

Before the problem occurs, you can allow your subconscious to help you. Enter a meditative frame of mind and **ask** your subconscious what is wrong. Your subconscious will give you clear answers and will explain where the problem is coming from and what you can do about it. Your problem probably has some very important things it would like to say to you, so pay attention to what your subconscious tells you. It always speaks the truth, and will tell you things that you might not like to hear but that you need to know.

When you become more aware of the potential problem you're beginning to create, you can change your thoughts and feelings, and, depending on what you decide to do about it, you can solve the problem before it actually becomes a problem. It's much easier to take care of a potential problem, but some people insist on creating full-fledged problems.

At this point, you know how to resolve the potential problem. But for any variety of reasons, some of which are perfectly good and valid, you may decide to let the potential problem manifest in your life. You may not be ready to take care of it, or you might want to experience the full expression of the problem to learn from it and to understand yourself better in many positive ways. Sometimes we create problems as a way to force ourselves to grow and change.

I've also noticed that some people create problems because they like to talk about them, to commiserate with other people, or to make themselves feel important because they think their problems are worse than someone else's. Or they set up problems so they can moan and complain about them and *poor little me* themselves into the pits of negativity.

Another thing that some people seem to do is to create problems because their lives are boring and a problem puts pizazz into their lives and gives them something to do. Then, when they solve the problem, they have a sense of accomplishment. This can be a good learning experience if it teaches you how to direct your energy in a positive way and shows you how to do things in a more efficient manner.

Anyway, for better or for worse, once you've established a problem in your life, you can use the magical power of your mind to take care of it. By accepting and acknowledging the problem that now exists, you're giving yourself the choice and the chance to change it—the power to do something positive about it. When you decide to take positive action, your mind will come up with solutions. In your thoughts, feelings, imagination, dreams, and reveries, your mind will show you many ways to work things out.

Your subconscious isn't going to sit still and let you suffer. It likes you too much. It's going to offer you ideas and ways to understand yourself and to correct the problem—to change the energy of it. All you have to do is listen to what your mind has to say and see what the problem has to offer you. Then decide how you're going to take care of it; put your choice into action and watch the changes happen.

If you're facing a full-fledged problem there are lots of positive ways you can resolve it. First, change the word *problem* to *challenge* or *opportunity*. This puts your perspective of the situation on a positive level. Challenges are so much more fun than problems. A challenge gives you something positive to do and inspires positive action, which in turn produces positive results. Second, see what it has to offer you. Look for all the opportunities within the problem. More often than not, you'll realize that what you thought was a problem is really a golden opportunity.

If you still want to hang on to your perception of a problem or if it appears to be unchangeable, you can use the problem to solve the problem. Change your perception of the problem and find a way to use it in a positive manner. One of my students wasn't getting enough sleep because her husband snored so loudly. Her marriage was beginning to suffer, she wasn't as productive on her job as she knew she could be, and she was tired and crabby all the time. She decided to use the sound of his snoring to lull her into a peaceful, deep, refreshing sleep. She gave herself positive suggestions to this effect and after a few nights, she was sleeping like a baby.

It comes down to where you direct your energy and how you perceive your problem. If a problem is emotionally painful or has become serious, you can detach yourself from it for a time. Step back from it to gain a bigger, better perspective, an overall picture. This allows you to be objective about it while giving you more information. Pretend the problem belongs to someone else and give that someone else some good advice. Then take that same advice to heart and solve your problem.

Another way to take care of a problem is to make it into an interactive movie. Imagine a Magical Mental Movie Screen in your mind and watch your problem for a while. Then, whenever you feel like it, get involved with it. Jump into your movie and make choices and changes to see what happens. If you don't like what plays out, change the scene. You can jump in and out whenever you want to. You can be an observer or a participant, or both at the same time. (This method is covered more completely in the next chapter.)

A fun way to solve a problem is to play with it. Open up your imagination and let it run free. Use reveries (self-guided visualizations) or fantasies to help you solve a problem. This is similar to your interactive movie. Play with the problem in all directions to see what happens and how you feel about each outcome.

With mind movies and reveries, you're doing more than just using your imagination. You're using the magical power of your mind, allowing your natural psychic abilities to give you accurate information and insight and to offer you guidance and direction in how to solve the problem. In addition to using the intuitive powers of your mind, you're also using your precognitive abilities to look into the future and to change things now in the present if you choose, so that the future happens just the way you want it to.

You can also use this method when you want to reach a decision about something or if you have choices and you're wondering what to do. For instance, suppose you've been offered a new job that seems great, but you like your present job. Mind movies and reveries can help you discover more information so you can determine what you really want to do.

Along those same lines, you can dream your problems away. If you have a problem you'd like to solve—one that you've decided to do something about but you're not quite sure what to do or how to do it—you can program a dream to show you what to do, or the dream itself can solve the problem for you (see Chapter Ten).

The very best way to solve a problem is to develop your own ways to solve it. You know better than anyone else what to do for yourself and how to do it. Listen to the little voice that whispers within. Open up the power of your mind and turn your problems into positive experiences!

On the shadow side of problems lurks fear. Sometimes people will set up problems as a way to cover up or work through a fear. A problem seems to be easier to deal with than a fear, and by resolving a problem it could be that you're being very brave and facing a fear. All of the problem-solving methods discussed earlier in this chapter work just as well for fears, and the following methods for understanding and overcoming fears can also solve problems.

You can take care of your fear before it becomes a fear. If you hold on to a feeling of fear strongly enough, it **will** become a fact; it will turn into a physical reality. Your fears can become self-fulfilling prophecies. Whatever you fear or worry about, you cause to come into existence because you're directing your energy toward that fear by thinking about it. You energize and activate the fear by imagining terrible and dire things. Sooner or later, those terrible things do happen because you thought about them so much that you created them. By giving energy to your fears, you give them the power to control you and your actions.

Your subconscious mind and your body respond to a

potential fear in exactly the same way they respond to a tangible fear. To show you how this works, close your eyes and remember when you were really afraid of something. Reexperience it, clearly and completely, in your mind. Remember your feelings and your thoughts. Remember how scared you were. Think about it for a few minutes, then open your eyes and let that thought go.

Just by recalling that event, your heart probably beat a little faster. Maybe your palms got sweaty and emotions relating to the fear surfaced. And all you did was remember something that frightened you, something that no longer exists. Your mind and your body responded to your thought by acting as if that fear were occurring right now, when, in reality, it was a past event.

Fears are crippling and hold you back from being truly positive and happy. Fear, or any negative emotion, uses up a tremendous amount of energy and drains you. Once you allow any negative emotion to be in control of you, it takes a while for you to return to a positive frame of mind. When you operate with fear as your companion, you have to expend twice the amount of energy necessary to get half as far as you could without that heavy burden of fear.

Have you ever noticed that when you have a really bad day or if you're worried about something, you feel exhausted and all you want to do is go to sleep? This is one of the magical ways that your mind helps you, because as you sleep, your subconscious works through the negativity for you in your dreams, sometimes without your being aware of it. You feel better when you wake up and your energy is replenished.

Whenever you're in a fear-producing situation, pay attention to your dreams. Your subconscious can help you overcome your fears through dreams. Sometimes your subconscious will show you a dream designed to scare you to help you face your fear. And just as often your subconscious, with its wonderful sense of humor, will show you a comedy to make you laugh at a fear or to put it into a manageable perspective. If your fear is deeply ingrained or you're not yet ready to face it directly, your subconscious will show you very special images or symbols for you to interpret based on your true feelings.

As long as you hold the same fears, you'll continue to experience negative events in your life relating to that fear until you take care of it. An easy way to overcome your fears is to simply let go of them. You're only bound to a fear by the thoughts you hold about it, so **cancel** those thoughts out! Fears can only exist if you give them the energy to exist. When you let go of that negative energy, you automatically replace the fear with positive thoughts and feelings.

REALITY CHECK: If you try to eliminate your fear by repressing it or ignoring it in the hopes that it will go away, or you try to resolve it by running away from it or refusing to deal with it, you'll be creating the proverbial bogeyman who will come back to haunt you. By ignoring a fear or running away from it, you're giving it even more energy to exist, and you'll actually cause your fear to become worse because you're not acknowledging and accepting your feelings. It's a very positive thing to feel fear. It's one of the things that keeps you alive and safe, and that rush of adrenaline is a super burst of energy that you can use to help you.

Call your courage into action. Stand up to your fear. Show it how powerful you are. Look your fear right in the eye; maybe you can scare it. This puts you on equal ground with your fear and it no longer controls you; you can take charge of it.

A very close friend of mine felt overwhelmed by some traumatic childhood memories that were trying to surface. She'd blocked them for most of her life and was terrified of looking into these memories; she wasn't sure what she'd find. Being a brave soul, she was determined to deal with them and overcome them. Over a period of time she employed imagery and reveries to help her uncover and face her fears. In her first reverie she saw a wolf growling and baring its teeth at her, and she thought this wolf represented all her fears. Then she noticed that the wolf was watching and waiting to see what she'd do. Although frightened of him, she edged closer and finally reached out and petted him. She put a leash on him, gave him a name, and began to walk with him through all her fearful childhood memories. The wolf became her guardian and her friend, preventing her fears from attacking her by scaring them and holding them at bay until she felt ready to take care of them, one by one.

If you feel overpowered by your fear or if it's very frightening, you can use the universal energies of white light to replenish your energy, to protect you, and to encourage and empower you. Envision yourself surrounded with white light. Breathe it inside you as you feel it all around you. White light will fill you with pure, positive energy and keep you safe in any situation as you work through your fear. There's a magical, mystical essence to it, and it is always available for any reason or purpose.

Note: What you're actually doing by calling white light to protect you is calling your own spiritual/universal energies into action. Sometimes people perceive white light as something outside of themselves, rather than within themselves, because they aren't yet ready to accept or believe in the awesome power of their mind. However you perceive white light, it works wonderfully well.

You can also use white light to illuminate your fear, to help you see it clearly. It's interesting that when you shine a light on something, the light illuminates the shadows, and the shadows disappear. More often than not, when you face your fear directly, you dissipate its energy and it disappears, somehow *magically* all by itself.

A nice, clean way to take care of a fear is to wash your fear away. Look at your fear as you would look at something dirty that you want to clean. If you were dirty because you'd been pulling weeds out of your garden, you'd take a shower and wash all the dirt away. So pull those weeds out of your subconscious mind. Take a good look at them. When you cleanse a fear, you acknowledge it directly and allow yourself to feel the fear wash over you; then it's no longer a fear because you've understood it and cleansed yourself of it.

Note: In cleansing a fear, you may experience that fear on an intense level for a short time because you've brought it up to the surface and you're dealing with it openly. This is natural, but don't jump out of the shower because all the dirt is coming off. Just use more soap.

If you'd prefer a less direct, but equally effective method, detach yourself from your fear and talk to it. Ask the fear questions and listen, really listen, to the answers. Allow it to tell you how it originated, why you created it, what purpose it served in the past and the purpose it serves now. Ask what it can help you learn or understand and what you can do to resolve it in a positive manner.

Fear is a friend who is just "inside out" for the moment. Turn your fears around; allow them to work *for* you rather than *against* you. Accept your fear as an opportunity or a challenge to know yourself better. Acknowledge it as a chance for positive change and inner growth. Fear as an enemy will hold you back. Fear as a friend will guide you as you move forward. It's your choice. You're the one with the power to make changes.

MIND-POWER EXERCISES

The following exercises are suggestions that you can use if you feel ready to work through a problem or a fear. If an exercise resonates with you, it's probably one that can turn out to be very helpful.

1. Become aware of potential problems in your life. Tune into why you're creating them. Once you understand why, write down your insights and use the information you gain to solve each problem before it becomes a problem. Note how you've changed your thoughts and feelings.

2. Take an inventory of the problems that exist now in your life. Write down what they have to offer you and what you're learning from them. Note all the opportunities you see within the problem. Then use the information to help yourself in any way you choose.

3. Make friends with a fear. Write down your fear and how you feel about it. This helps you acknowledge it and accept it. Then explore that fear. Discover how you can allow it to help you. Find the best and most positive way for you to deal with your fear. Play with a reverie or engage in a dialogue with your subconscious or watch a magical mind movie to view images and feelings. Do whatever feels right for you to make friends with your fear. Listen to yourself and trust your feelings. Write down how you've turned your fear around and how you feel about it now.

4. Look at the seemingly negative situations that are showing up as problems or fears and let these situations show you how to be happy and how to experience everything in your life as being positive.

CHAPTER SIX

Subconscious Scripts

Being a positive person doesn't mean that negative events will never happen to you again. Being a positive person means that you have the ability and power to experience all aspects of your life in a positive way.

One of the biggest blocks to being truly happy and positive is *un*conscious negativity. *Un*happiness is often a result of your *un*conscious, *un*aware mind. The way to remove that block is to look within yourself to uncover negative influences that govern your present experiences. You can open up and correct those negative influences by becoming conscious of them and changing your perception of them.

When negativity rears its ugly little head, people tend to give all their power away by pushing the experience away from them or by blaming someone or something else for it, rather than face the negativity and deal directly with it. Unaccepted and unconscious negativity can surface to sabotage any and all efforts on your part to fully open up the magical power of your mind and your mystical awareness and can numb you to your spiritual nature. This negativity needs to be reframed and reprogrammed into a positive awareness.

It's time to take all the garbage out and joyfully dump the burdens that weigh heavily on your mind so you can live your life in a happy, positive way. It's as easy as shrugging your shoulders and letting all the negativity slide away. But watch out for the side effects.

Your conscious and subconscious awareness must be in agreement with your unconscious perceptions. You can try to tell yourself that nothing is wrong and everything is positive, but you can't fool your subconscious. If your perceptions about your experiences are not in agreement in all levels of your mind, an inner conflict is created and expresses itself in negative ways until the issue is resolved.

For instance, suppose something awful happens to you and you decide to forget about it because you don't want the negativity around you. You'll be creating an inner conflict because you're repressing the experience instead of working through it and understanding it, and changing your perceptions of it so that the experience becomes a positive one.

Inner conflicts are also created when your emotions surface without the corresponding memory of an earlier event. This happens when the memory is painful or traumatic. You unconsciously block the memory, but you can't block the feelings associated with it. If you've ever wondered why you react in an uncharacteristic or unusual way in certain situations, you're probably responding to an unconscious memory.

Whatever that memory is, it isn't consciously dealt with, so you unconsciously create distractions or other ways for your feelings to be expressed. Your feelings can show up as problems, or fears, or as sickness and/or dis-ease (see Chapter Twelve), or in repeated negative experiences. This shows you that you're responding unconsciously to the memory. The memory is in control of you, rather than you being in control of it.

Your subconscious tries to help you understand and work through these unconscious conflicts in the best way it can, most often through your feelings and dreams. But every now and then your subconscious would like a helping hand from you. The place to start is by seeing through the symbology in your experiences. This helps you find the underlying cause and brings it into your conscious mind, where you can correct the experience. The next step is to accept responsibility for all your experiences, which you created by your choices (some of them unconsciously). This gives you the power to change your experiences.

One of the things I've noticed is that sometimes people, in order to change something deeply unconscious and negative, feel they need to make themselves unhappy to help them realize that a change is necessary. Being a positive person and having a positive and beautiful life can be so much better when you come from happiness to create even more happiness.

One of the culprits in unconscious negativity is those irritating voices that you hear in your thoughts. The voices that berate and belittle you. The voices that you know don't belong to you but that you can't seem to shut up or turn off. So they play, over and over again, like a worn-out tape recording that says things that aren't true and probably never were.

Some of those negative voices may belong to your childhood peers who taunted you and made fun of you. Others may belong to your parents, teachers, and other people who were controlling authority figures. You may have believed every word they said. Your acceptance of their words, opinions, and actions formed your early frame of reference and also wrote the subconscious scripts that may no longer be applicable, but even as an adult, you're still listening to them and responding unconsciously to their negative programming. As you grew into adolescence and adulthood, all the *shoulds*, *coulds*, and *woulds* along the way probably also influenced your frame of reference. Maybe people told you how you *should* feel about certain things when you felt differently, or they told you that you *could* have done something better when you know you did your best, or maybe they said that things *would* have been different if circumstances had been different.

As you become more positive in your life, you may find that your earlier programming, which created your patterns of behavior and response, is causing inner conflicts that express themselves in negative experiences. You can see these patterns by the way you now respond to the people and situations in your life. For example, maybe you always have rotten relationships or you can't seem to accomplish something you truly want. If all your efforts bring the same results, no matter what you do or how positively you do it, then an unconscious, negative pattern is probably being played out. Until you consciously change the recordings to reflect your present positive attitude, they'll continue to influence you and to play out the same messages, and you'll unconsciously create negative experiences to correspond with them.

Listen to the voices carefully to see who they belong to and what they say. When you recognize who the voices belong to, your feelings will tell you whether those voices have any validity with you now. If their messages are no longer appropriate, you can change the tape by changing your perceptions and rewriting the scripts.

One of those voices will probably sound very familiar because it belongs to you. It's the negative, nagging voice of your gremlin speaking to you from the shadow side of your mind. We all have an inner critic. He's a nasty little bugger, and he could be the culprit who echoes your negative subconscious scripts. Maybe he's the one who pushes the buttons and plays the old worn-out recordings to you. He could be the one who parades your negative feelings in your unconscious mind and throws negative experiences into your life.

Also consider the possibility that your subconscious scripts could be habits that you've become so accustomed to that you don't give them a second thought. It might be a good idea to think twice about the ruts and routines you may be stuck in. If a habit doesn't suit you anymore, you can find new approaches and alternatives to an outdated way of doing things.

Changing habits, rewriting subconscious scripts or rearranging the way you respond to them, and reversing unconscious voices most often occur in stages over a period of time, though they can be done instantaneously. Perhaps you've had a habit of doing something or listening and responding to those voices for twenty years. It seems logical, although limiting, to assume that they can't be changed in twenty minutes—**unless you use the magical power of your mind to change your perceptions.**

It's helpful, though not absolutely necessary, to get back to the beginning—to clearly understand early events so you can rewrite or change any negative programming. By becoming consciously aware of these events and changing your perceptions of what originally occurred, you can also change the energy vibrations of a past event and the way that energy is expressed now. You have the power to change the past event into a positive experience.

Changing an unconscious negative pattern requires a conscious effort. To effectively and permanently rewrite both your unconscious and subconscious scripts or change a habit, you must truly *want* to change, *believe* that a change is possible, and *know* that it will occur. Your positive words, thoughts, and feelings, combined with the magical power of your imagination, will rearrange the wording in your unconscious recordings and change any habit or pattern that you want to change.

Changing your perceptions occurs in a gentle way by allowing yourself to replace or rearrange the energy of the negativity with a positive perception of it by centering your attention on the positive aspects of the events, rather than the negative ones. It consists of looking into the memory to see the purpose it served and the benefits you gained from having that experience. There may still be a wonderfully positive purpose in there that only needs to be viewed in a different manner.

If you'd prefer not to open up a past memory, you can take care of the negative expressions of it every time it shows up in your life by repeating positive affirmations that counteract what the negativity is saying. For example, if you have recurring, similar experiences that seem to denigrate your feelings of self-worth, you can repeat an appropriate positive affirmation that shows your present belief in your feelings of worthiness. Soon the repetitive affirmation will replace what the negative, unconscious voice says. You'll be overwriting your subconscious scripts. This method also requires a diligent conscious effort.

There are many ways to reframe your perceptions. Your subconscious will show you the most effective way for you to see how, why, and where past patterns originated, to see what purpose they served in the past and the purpose they serve now. Enter a meditative frame of mind and follow your feelings to find the best way for you to become aware of past memories that are negatively influencing you now. As you become aware of the memories, you'll instinctively and intuitively know how to rewrite your subconscious scripts and change the way you respond to unconscious programming.

If you'd like, you can read through and then do the following meditation to see what information you become aware of, or you can come up with a do-it-yourself meditation written exclusively and specifically for you by your magical mind.

The meditation I've written is general in nature and consists of watching a movie on the Magical Mental Movie Screen in your mind. This can give you wonderful insights into your previous experiences. Perhaps you've already done something like this when you worked on a problem or a fear. Before you do this meditation, do some serious thinking. Think about an experience or a feeling in your life that strongly indicates that an unconscious, negative past pattern is being expressed. Select something you'd like to understand and change. Give your movie a title, a few words that show a symbolic summary of what you've decided to work on.

Most important, before you begin, let go of the limiting belief that the past cannot be changed. It *can* be changed, and you have the power within you to change anything you choose.

This movie is all about you. It flows simultaneously between the past and the present. You control the picture, what you view and experience, and the way you experience it. You control whether you're in the scene experiencing it, or above the scene watching it. If anything painful or traumatic comes up as the past plays out, you—as an adult now—can nurture your younger self in a loving way to help you see and understand the memory that will ultimately be very healing for you. Because you're directing the movie and this is your life, you can rewrite and reframe the past so that it reflects your positive past/present perception of any event.

The movie begins in the present, goes into the past to show you the origins of the negativity, then lets you reframe the pictures from the past by changing your perceptions and rewriting earlier events. The movie then brings those changes into the present and shows how your positive past changes affect your experiences now.

Imagine that you're in a movie theater about to watch a movie all about your life—a movie that will show you scenes of earlier events that are important for you to become aware of. You may hear other voices as well as your own as you see and reenact the original drama to uncover the causes of and to look for positive aspects inside your earlier experiences. As the movie begins, the title flashes across the screen and you see yourself as you are now. You're watching a scene that depicts what you'd like to change.

The movie begins to run in reverse to the point of origin. As the movie goes back slowly through time, you see images of events that are relevant to the original scene. These highlights give you insight into your present experiences and show how you've unconsciously responded to earlier events.

And now you're there, in the past, where it began and you see the memory clearly. But it isn't a memory anymore; it's happening for the first time. The past and the present are simultaneous, silhouetted upon one another. You see how the pattern began, how it influenced your life then, and how it influences your experiences now, and you understand how and why the pattern began and what made you accept it.

As you become aware of this information, you realize that you have the power to re-create this scene in a different way by changing your feelings and perceptions about it. As you re-create the events and reexperience them in a new way, the movie screen glows with a luminous, bluish-white light. A soft blur of images plays in

*your mind as you change your perceptions—as you shape
and mold and create the images of past events to reflect
a positive experience. And now those changed images
come clearly into focus, showing the positive changes
you've made, both in your mind and your feelings, and
in the actual events.*

*The movie begins to slowly run forward, returning to
the present. It shows the scenes along the way as they flow
from the past into the present, reflecting the changes
you've made.*

*And now you see the opening scene again, but it's dif-
ferent now. It shows your understanding and insights; it
shows the changes you've made through your positive
perceptions of earlier events.*

*The movie goes on to show you how you can incor-
porate the changes you've made into your life; it shows
you your new responses to situations where a positive pattern now emerges from past events. As the movie comes
to a close, you know that it's up to you to put those positive changes into effect in your life now.*

When you're done with this meditation, take your
time to completely understand everything you've seen
and become aware of, knowing that your subconscious
has shown you a magical movie that allowed you to
change more than pictures; it allowed you to change your
life—to become truly happy and positive in everything
you do.

But watch out for a sudden shock just inside your conscious mind. A side effect just popped into the picture. Here comes your gremlin, ready to pounce on the positive changes you've just made. Chances are you already know your gremlin. You've met him many times before, probably in disguise, and he may have appeared in your movie. For the sake of clarity, we'll refer to your gremlin as "him." I'd like to formally introduce you to him and present a personality profile because, to be quite honest and realistic, you're stuck with him. He's been with you forever and is the negative or shadow side of you. Another term for this little bugger is your inner critic.

Your gremlin is most famous for robbing you of time and energy. He makes you fall asleep every time you try to meditate or he keeps you up all night worrying about things that you know you've already taken care of. He's the one who is constantly babbling and running off at the mouth with your conscious mind chatter.

He makes mundane things like laundry and grocery shopping seem more important than they really are. He insists that they have to get done NOW when you're doing something more fun or magical and you have plenty of time to do them later. He gives you headaches and makes you believe you have to go to the doctor when you're perfectly healthy.

Quite often, he'll attack you with a case of the blahs, depression, boredom, or negativity. His favorite thing in life is to squelch your positive attitude, and his main purpose is to make you doubt yourself and the magical power of your mind. If you don't obtain instantaneous and remarkable results the first time you try something, he'll tell you that you're a failure.

He invented Murphy's Law ("If anything can go wrong, it will, and at the worst possible time."). He lives and breathes by it, and tries to enforce it on you and make you believe it, too.

His appetite is voracious and he feeds off your negativity, fear, doubt, worry, anxieties, problems, etc. Breakfast for him usually consists of starting your day off totally wrong. When you wake up, he'll tell you to go back to sleep. He's usually very convincing, giving you lots of positive-sounding reasons for sleeping five more minutes. He tells you that you'll have more energy, you'll feel better, and you'll have a better day. You oversleep by an hour, which really makes him happy. You rush around the house trying to get ready (this is where the extra energy comes in). You don't have time for breakfast, you're late for work, and you have a totally rotten day, all because you listened to him in the first place. He's not concerned. He's already had his breakfast, and he's full of you-know-what!

He likes to disguise negative words as positive words. He uses words like *hope* and *attempt*, as well as the more obvious ones like *should*, *can't*, *won't*, and so on and so forth. He especially likes to use double negatives in the same sentence.

He'll fog up the magical mirror in your mind so you

can't clearly see your true self-image. When you smile at yourself in the mirror, he'll grimace at you in return.

He'll try to convince you it's OK to do something that you don't want to do, like cheat on your diet. He summons up visions of hot fudge sundaes and says, "One little bite won't hurt you." Then he says, "Wow, that was really good. Why don't you eat the whole thing and come back for seconds?"

It seems that he can influence circumstances. He'll give you a flat tire when you have to be somewhere important. If you're a writer, he'll break your computer or make your software go buggy two days before deadline.

Sometimes, just as you come up with the perfect solution to a problem, he causes a big disturbance and distracts you. Or just as you're recalling a fragmented dream and putting the pieces of it together and beginning to understand it, he'll make the phone ring. It's almost always a wrong number. He'll find a way to lure you away from solving your problems or recalling your dreams and make you lose your memories of them. Then he tells you to tell yourself that you'll never remember, what's the use, I give up!

Is he beginning to sound familiar yet?

He loves to make you run around in circles doing the same thing over and over and telling you that you'll never get it right. He scatters your thoughts and energies by trying to make you think of too many things at once or by giving you too many things to do at the same time. This causes you to feel frazzled and frustrated to the point where you can't keep your thoughts clear, and then you're stuck in his home territory and he's got full reign over you.

He likes to give you advice, which always turns out to be a bum steer. When he gets you to do something negative, he jumps up and down with absolute glee and you can usually feel this in the pit of your stomach.

He'll screw up the balance in your checkbook so you think you have more money than you really do. He'll tell you to treat yourself to something you either know you can't afford or don't really want. He gets very bubbly when all your checks start bouncing, and you usually experience this as gas.

He does have a few good characteristics. He's not lazy. He's got lots of energy (negative), and he's stubborn, persistent, and determined (to get in your way). Every once in a while—rarely—he tries to be nice. He'll remind you that you have to be at the dentist three hours after you've missed your appointment. Or he makes excuses for you and these excuses seem to be very reasonable, but his excuses always begin with the word *but*.

Another thing he's famous for is laying guilt trips on you. If you decide to take a well-earned day off from work just to lay around and enjoy yourself, he'll try all sorts of tricks to ruin your day. He'll make you worry about things at work and will insist that this is a perfect day to mow the lawn, clean out the garage, and vacuum your dirty rugs.

I could go on forever, but you get the general drift. Since you've been turning negatives into positives and you're applying the magical power of your mind in your life, he probably hasn't bothered you for a while, but that's because he's been in hiding, regrouping for another attack. He only wanted you to think you've won the war while he was busy planning and preparing for another battle.

Remember that you've had the same amount of time to gather and strengthen your inner resources. You've been exercising your mental muscles and restructuring your positive frame of mind. His worst enemies and your best friends are a positive attitude, happiness, and belief in yourself as the truly magical person that you are.

He resides in a dark dungeon just inside of your conscious mind. He likes to think that he guards the gates to your subconscious like a troll, and to get into a positive frame of mind, you have to bypass him—but you know this isn't true, and he knows it, too. He still hopes you'll fall for it, though, and tries to exact a heavy price of negativity from you to let you through.

Now would be a good time for you to meet your gremlin face to face. Just look for a shadow lurking outside your positive thoughts and grab your gremlin by the hand. You'll probably have to drag him, resisting and screaming, into a meditative frame of mind in order to properly introduce yourself and to tell him that you're the boss.

Meeting your gremlin is an entertaining and enlightening experience. Your subconscious likes to play, so have a good time with this. Once you meet him, see what your gremlin looks like and how you feel about him. Find out what his name is. The name is usually symbolic and so is his appearance. You can talk to your gremlin.

Gremlins are very articulate, but sometimes they'll be silent, trying to make you guess what they're thinking. And beware: they like to play mind games to confuse you. Just remember that you're smarter and more powerful than your gremlin is. You're magical and he isn't.

Now that you've met him and you know more about your gremlin, there are lots of positive ways you can deal with this little critic whenever he pops up in your life or tries to get the better of you. By the way, he's only about two feet tall. He can't survive in a positive atmosphere for more than a few minutes. When you recognize him and see him for what he is, he can't stand that either. He'll run away screaming, like you've really hurt him. That's designed to make you feel guilty. He's surrounded in shadows; shine a light on him, then he disappears. Use your imagination to put him in a positive place. He hates that. Sometimes I laugh at what my gremlin is doing to me because he can be quite humorous. This really bothers him because he knows I've seen through him. If you give him something positive to do, he'll give you a dirty look and make nasty comments, but he'll leave you alone entirely.

MIND-POWER EXERCISES

If you continue to experience negative events that you seem to have no control over, the following Mind-Power Exercises might be beneficial.

1. Write down the way your reframing and rescripting of the movie showed itself. You'll know whether the reframing was effective because of your feelings and because of what you begin to experience in your life. If you want to or need to, re-view your movie again—maybe from a different perspective—to see if there's anything you might have missed the first time or to dig even deeper into your unconscious.

2. If you experience any negative feelings or situations that you'd like to know more about, pretend that you're a newspaper reporter and write a story on it. Include who, what, where, when, why, and how. Interview the negativity and notice any judgments or labels you put on the experience. Write the story from two different perspectives, from an objective and a subjective viewpoint. This will help you become aware of how you consciously feel about the experience and how you unconsciously respond to it, and can also help you resolve an inner conflict.

3. Think about a habit you'd like to change and why you'd like to change it. Write down how and why you feel your habit began, what purpose it served in the past, and the purpose it serves for you now. Enter a meditative frame of mind to see how you'll change it, then put that change into motion. See yourself changing it and visualize your results. Look at all the positive benefits you'll receive in return for changing this habit. Pay attention to any symbology or special insights you become aware of. These provide you with a positive direction to pursue and can prove to be very helpful hints for you to follow.

4. If your gremlin pops up in your life from time to time, and he will, listen to what he says. See through the negativity in his words. Sometimes, without meaning to, he'll tell you things that can lead you to a wonderful insight that will help you understand yourself better. Notice when he pops up and why. Look into your feelings or the circumstances or the situation that causes him to appear. This can help you change your feelings or your perceptions about those situations.

5. No matter what happens in your life, be positive about it and realize that the negativity is there to help you, not hinder you. Everything happens for a good reason or a higher purpose, which may not be immediately apparent on the surface. Look for the positives and the opportunities within all your experiences. It's easy to see now that you know what to look for. Let the magical power of your mind help you to become perfectly positive in every avenue and aspect of your life.

PART II
SPIRITUALITY

You've come a long way from your comfy chair where you first colored rainbows. Are you ready to continue on the rainbow path that leads you within, and to find your own special place in the sun, where you can be the positive, magical, spiritual person that you really are and always were?

CHAPTER SEVEN

Your Imagination and Your Inner Self

You already know that your mind speaks to you in images rather than words. The thoughts you hear and the pictures you see in your mind originate in your imagination—the magical world of your inner images. Your imagination is where you can rediscover the real you, where you can be totally free to simply be who you really are. It's where you can reconnect with your true spiritual nature.

Until now, maybe you've thought that only what you perceive with your conscious mind is what is real. While this is true, that's just half of it. There's another world that's also very real and is waiting to show you what's within yourself. It may seem that reality only revolves around your conscious mind and your physical senses, but it also continually swirls through your subconscious awareness, coming up to the surface and showing itself in your thoughts and ideas, your feelings, and your dreams. Maybe you've had experiences where an answer or an insight sparkled into your mind out of the clear blue sky, where your inner, spiritual self was whispering to you through your thoughts and intuition. And perhaps there were times where a dream was unusually clear and vivid—a dream that seemed to be more than just a dream.

Intellectually and intuitively, you're aware of both your conscious and subconscious perceptions. In the everyday work world and just taking care of life in general, we tend to clutter up our thoughts with meaningless mind chatter and mundane things, and we often bury our real feelings under layers of mask and pretense. We're so surrounded by physical chaos and noise, and the *should*s that society imposes upon us, that we don't pay attention to our more subtle, inner sense of awareness. We're so busy scattering our thoughts and energies and running around doing things that we can't even hear ourselves think. Underneath the facade of what we call reality is the true real world— the real us.

Once we let go of outside distractions and tune into our subconscious, we can be in touch with ourselves and see that our inner self and our higher self are one and the same. We can bring that inner, more perceptive awareness of our true spiritual nature into our everyday world and know what's really happening beneath the hustle and bustle. We can be in both worlds simultaneously. When we take the time to relax—to just be natural, to be who we really are, to just *be*—we're able to direct our attention into a quiet, gentle part of ourselves. There, we can listen to our thoughts and allow our feelings to speak clearly. We can look at what we hear and know the true awareness of our spirit.

So come and explore this magical world of your imagination and watch your mystical mind in motion. You may see that your imagination is more real than you think it is. And you may be in for a few surprises as you reconnect with your inner self and reunite with your higher self—the one who speaks to you through your feelings, the one who whispers spiritual knowledge into your mind.

Just by stretching your imagination and opening up your mind, you can become so much more aware of the worlds within you and around you. Reality is more than it appears to be on the surface and your imagination will show this to you. Take some time for yourself and relax. Read through the following mind-opening meditation, then close your eyes and imagine that you're there. It's as easy as believing it to be so. Let your magical mind be your guide through the world of your inner images. Somewhere inside yourself, you'll touch your true feelings and rediscover the magic of the real you—the magic of your inner spiritual self. And if you listen, you'll be able to hear a voice that whispers to you—your inner voice that's real and true, the voice that always speaks the truth.

Imagine a very pleasant, warm summer day. You remember when you first walked through the rainbow and began to discover the magical power of your mind, and now you're ready to travel further along that path that leads you within. You know the rainbow is there in the sunshine, somewhere. You decide to go for a walk through nature, to feel connected with the earth, to appreciate the beauty and experience the joy and harmony of the earth with the universe. Deep inside you, you know that you're part of that special connection and you'd like to feel that again.

The day is filled with the quiet sounds of nature; you can feel and hear the gentle breeze as it touches you and moves softly through the leaves of the trees in the forest just ahead of you. Walking toward the trees, you feel the warmth and energy of the sun and begin to experience a sense of aliveness and vibrancy that being in nature brings you. Breathing in deeply, you feel the pure, clean air circulate through your lungs, revitalizing and rejuvenating you. As universal energy flows through your body, you feel lighter and happier. All your cares and worries slip away as you enjoy this beautiful day, this wonderful walk through nature.

As you follow the path that leads you within, you enter the forest. The sunshine sparkles through the tops of the trees, creating patterns and playing with shafts of light on the forest floor. You notice how intricate the patterns are and how they're constantly moving and changing. As you walk through the open, airy forest, it feels as if you're walking on a soft bed of earth.

You notice how quiet it is inside the forest, and how peaceful it is. You begin to enter a meditative frame of mind—a special, serene place within yourself where you feel completely comfortable and natural. You see a clearing up ahead and the sunlight beckons you forth, welcoming you. You know that you've been here before—in your thoughts and in your dreams. Feeling perfectly at home and in tune with yourself, you walk slowly, thoughtfully into the clearing. There you sit quietly on the soft ground for a few minutes, just enjoying the feeling of peace and harmony, both within you and all around you.

The gentle breeze creates a light, musical sound that vibrates in harmony within your mind as the wind blows softly through the leaves of the trees. Leaning up against a tree, you close your eyes, listening to your thoughts and watching their images move in your mind.

The leaves whisper in the wind and through your mind, sharing the secrets of nature with anyone who will listen. Somehow you know that you can communicate with the tree, and you listen as it tells you about its connection with the earth and the universe, about how its roots are connected to the earth as its branches reach toward the sky, toward the universe. It speaks to you of the harmony that is within nature, the harmony that the earth and the universe share, the harmony that you share between your physical self and your spiritual self. It tells you that the universe is within you and that you are the universe, expressing yourself in earthly form.

After a while, you open your eyes. Looking up at the sky, you see a few puffy white clouds floating leisurely by and you notice how blue and expansive the sky is. It seems to go on forever, beyond the horizon into the universe and even farther than that into infinity. The sky has an ethereal quality—a magical, mystical essence that you can't quite describe with words—a majesty that you've known before but haven't experienced for a while. Breathing in deeply, you absorb the depth of the blueness within yourself; the color fills you with a wonderful sense of inner peace and awareness.

Standing up, you feel as if you could reach up through the sky and touch the universe. Stretching your arms in an open embrace toward the sky, you feel a magical surge of energy and power inside you, knowing that you're part of the earth and the universe. You sense how awesome the world really is, and you begin to rediscover how awesome you really are; you begin to sense your true spiritual nature and the higher power within you.

You decide to continue walking, to explore everything you see, and to experience and understand both the world within you and the world around you. Your pace is slower now, more in rhythm and harmony with your mind's awareness that is beginning to open up completely.

Reaching the edge of the forest, you see a field of flowers growing wild and free in a meadow. As you walk through them, you sense how truly alive the flowers are;

you sense how special and magical they are. Breathing in their wonderful fragrance, you sense their inner essence and you become aware of how they're connected to both the earth and the universe, just as you are.

You know they're vibrantly alive, flowing with the natural energy of life, and you know that you're even more vibrantly alive. You begin to run, to express your awareness opening up inside you and to feel your own spiritual energy vibrating inside your physical body. As you run joyfully through the meadow, totally experiencing and enjoying your freedom and energy, you feel the wind in your hair and the gentle warmth of the sun on your face. You feel as if you're a child again, free and completely happy.

Ahead of you, the meadow turns into a gently sloping valley. As you slow down and look into the valley, you see how green and healthy and beautiful everything is. The sun radiates sparkles of light from a softly winding stream of water in the center, and you hear the sound of a waterfall. As you stop and listen to the sound, you know that the waterfall is hidden just beyond the bushes and rocks that you see on your right.

Walking that way, you can smell the water and almost see a rainbow. Smiling to yourself, you know that the rainbow you see in your mind is real and that you've found the path that leads you within to your true spiritual self. Parting the bushes, you see a magnificent waterfall gush-

ing with life as it tumbles down. Every drop of water catches the sunlight and reflects a beautiful rainbow as the water cascades into a gentle, quiet pool beneath.

You follow the footpath down through the lush, flowering bushes to where the waterfall enters a clear, sparkling pool. As you kneel down to run your fingers through the water, you look into the pool and see more than the reflection of your physical self. Shimmering in the water is the essence of your inner spiritual self, moving around and through your image in gentle ripples. You notice how the water reflects and mirrors the sky above you, and as you recognize that your physical self is really a mirror of your spiritual self, you realize that the universe is within you.

And you know that the reality of your imagination goes much deeper than your conscious mind, much farther than the physical world. Below the surface and all around you in every experience, your subconscious awareness—your magical inner self, your mystical higher self— waits ever so quietly to be recognized, to be heard. As you fully open up your imagination—your mind—you hear your true inner voice whispering to you in your feelings and thoughts, and through your dreams and experiences. As you listen, you know you can feel and become completely aware of all the vibrations of all your experiences as you travel through them, following your rainbow path that leads you within to your magical, mystical mind.

MIND-POWER EXERCISES

1. Create a special place—a quiet, tranquil nature scene—in your mind that's all your own. A place where you feel completely comfortable and natural, where you enjoy being peaceful, calm, and happy within yourself. A magical place where you can truly be who you really are, where you can tune into your inner self and listen to your inner voice. A spiritual sanctuary where you can connect with your true spiritual nature and experience harmony within yourself, where you can open up the complete awareness of your mind.

Your nature scene can be a beach, where you can listen to the sound of the waves and watch them as they gently ebb and flow. It can be a forest, where you can hear the wind gently moving through the leaves in the trees, whispering to you. It can be a wide open expanse of earth, where you can view the horizon clearly in all directions. It can be a mountain or a valley. It can be a lake, where you can go sailing, or a wonderful waterfall. It can be a garden with very beautiful flowers. It can be a rainbow, it can be the sky, it can be the sun, or it can simply be the air that you breathe. Your nature scene can be wherever and whatever you want it to be.

It can be reminiscent of a place you've been before or it can be a place that you create entirely with your imagination. Think about the kind of place you'd like to have as your nature scene. Close your eyes and create a picture in your mind of the place that would make you most happy. When you've got a good picture in your mind, be there—create that scene. You may find an exact replica of your conscious thoughts or you may find that you create a different scene once you're inside the magical, mystical world of your imagination. Whatever you see and create is the most perfect nature scene for you.

When you've created your nature scene, just be there for a while to enjoy it and to appreciate nature. Tune into your feelings, reconnect with your inner self—your real spiritual self—and listen to your inner voice. Hear what it sounds like and how it speaks to you.

2. After you've been in your nature scene several times, notice how you feel when you're there, what you do and what you think about. Thoroughly explore your nature scene. Notice everything that's there. Notice any previous connections to pleasant and positive experiences in your life. See the symbology in it and what it represents to you by exploring your feelings about it. Become aware of why these connections are surfacing in your nature scene.

3. Aside from the obvious benefits of being able to go into your nature scene at any time to just relax for a few moments, to feel peace and harmony, to refresh and revitalize yourself, or to let go of stress and tension that may build up during your day, your nature scene gives you the opportunity to quietly reflect on the things that are happening in your life. You can look within yourself to see how and why your experiences originated. You can find solutions to problems and answers to any questions you pose. Listen to your inner voice, to your true feelings. Talk to your inner self—your higher self. Ask for guidance. Trust the information that comes from your inner knowledge and act on the information given.

4. Your nature scene is much more than it appears to be. It is truly a real, magical place within you that opens up into many wonderful worlds that offer you insight and understanding into yourself; worlds that open up into universal knowledge; worlds that show you your mystical mind—your spiritual essence. Explore those worlds.

CHAPTER EIGHT

Physical Senses

Your five physical senses are very special; maybe you've been taking them for granted and haven't been using them to their fullest potential. You probably use them without thinking about them, and your senses have become automatic and unconscious for you. For example, when you look at something, you're only aware of using your sense of sight, and your other senses are ignored even though you're using them at the same time. You're picking up much more information, but you're only consciously aware of the information received through your sense of sight. Subconsciously, though, you sense everything.

By focusing both your conscious and subconscious awareness into everything you experience, you can see every part of your life in a much more full and open way.

As you tune into the information and impressions you receive through all your senses and as you incorporate your subconscious awareness into your everyday experiences, you'll be more aware of everything you experience. By completely opening up and redeveloping your physical senses, you'll see how they're inextricably interwoven with each other.

When you use all your senses together, instead of separately, your experiences become a complete adventure that opens up into many avenues of awareness. You can take something mundane and make it magical simply by revitalizing your senses and focusing all your attention into your experiences.

Special moments aren't limited to experiences that are few and far between. They happen all the time. All you have to do is notice them. The more vividly you perceive and experience and become involved with something, the greater your awareness of the event or the sensation will be. By becoming more aware on a physical, sensory level, you'll also find that your natural abilities of psychic perception and spiritual awareness become more alive and energized within you. You can use these abilities in perfect harmony with your five physical senses every day, in every way, to make your life ever so much better as you explore and experience the true reality of things.

What you formerly perceived as regular, ordinary, everyday activities can become the special, magical experiences they truly are. When you completely immerse yourself in your experiences with all your five physical senses working together at peak performance, you can do so much more than see, hear, touch, taste, and smell.

In the following three-part exercise, you'll be exploring and rediscovering your five physical senses as the special senses they really are by elevating them to a level where you're completely aware and fully conscious of them. The more you become involved with the images and your feelings in experiencing the sensory details and descriptions, the more you'll open up the full range of your senses.

For the first part of this exercise, read through the following paragraphs one at a time. After you've read each paragraph, enter a meditative frame of mind to explore and experience the images and feelings that the words inspire. To begin with, focus on exploring each sense separately although you may find that several images are very vivid and invoke your other senses.

For this exercise, use your mind's eye to visualize and your inner sense of touch to feel. Rely on your memories of what all your senses have experienced as you open up and develop them to their fullest potential. Then transfer this awareness to everything you experience in your life, both consciously and subconsciously.

SIGHT. In addition to looking at something, use your sense of sight to really **see** things clearly, with both your mind's eye and your physical eyes. Bring all the visual images of what you're looking at within your mind so that everything you see is very detailed and clear. Allow your physical sense of sight to fully open up inside you. Remember when you saw a sunrise or a sunset. Remember something very beautiful. Remember when you saw something very colorful and bright. Remember a special person's face.

TOUCH. In addition to touching with your hands, use your sense of touch to really **feel**. Caress whatever you're touching with your hands and absorb the sensations within your mind. Remember when your hands were cold and what that felt like. Remember when your hands were very warm. Remember when your hands were wet. Remember when you felt something very soft. Something hard.

HEARING. In addition to hearing with your ears, use your sense of hearing to really **listen**. Pull the sounds within your mind and hear how they sound inside of you. Remember the sound of a clock ticking. Remember and listen to the sound the rain makes when it taps against a window. Remember the melody of your favorite song and listen to the words. Listen to the sound of your voice when you talk.

TASTE. In addition to tasting with your mouth, use your sense of taste to really **savor** with your mind. Remember and reexperience the flavors and textures of the food you ate for dinner. Remember when you tasted something sweet. Something sour. Remember the taste of your favorite food. Remember when you drank something cold. Something hot. Remember how it felt and tasted in your mouth.

SMELL. In addition to smelling with your nose, use your sense of smell to **breathe in** the aroma of the air around you and absorb it within your mind. Remember the smell of a flower. Remember the smell of something delicious cooking in your kitchen. Remember the scent of your favorite cologne. Remember the smell of a spring morning.

For the second part of this exercise, choose an item that seemed ordinary and uninteresting that you explored with one sense. Reexplore it, but this time focus your full attention into what you're experiencing with all your senses working together in a more aware manner. For example, the smell of a spring morning. Remember a time in the spring when the world was waking up from a winter's sleep and you were outside. Breathe in the fresh, clean scent of the air and enjoy the feeling of being alive on such a beautiful day. Feel the warmth of the sun on your face and your skin. Listen to the sounds you heard, perhaps the sound of birds chirping. Notice the dewdrops on the green grass; put a blade of grass in your mouth and taste it. Look at the early spring flowers in bloom and the buds on the trees and bushes. Touch them gently. Notice all the things you felt and saw and sensed as you enjoyed the smell of a spring morning. Bring them all together in your mind.

For the third part of this exercise, look around you at everyday items, really noticing and exploring with all your senses everything that is there. For example, pay attention to this book that you're holding in your hands. Notice the feel of the cover, the texture of the pages, and the size of the print. Smell the print on the pages. Notice the way the light shines on the page and see if there are any shadows. Look at the picture on the cover and the colors. Be aware of the chair you're sitting in and how you're sitting. Be aware of all the sights, smells, and sounds around you.

Perhaps you have a glass of iced tea or something else that you're sipping. If so, employ all of your senses together in a more aware and focused manner. Use them to look at and see, hear and listen to, touch and feel, taste and savor, and smell and breathe in the flavor of the iced tea. Perhaps there's a lemon wedge floating at the top, maybe with a big seed in the center. Look at and see the color of the tea. Is it light or dark? What kind of glass is it in? Notice if there's moisture on the outside of the glass. Touch the glass, feel the coolness and wetness with your hand. Listen to and hear the sound the ice cubes make as they clink against the glass and one another. Smell and breathe in the aroma of the tea. What kind of tea is it? Take a sip; taste and savor how good the tea is. Is it sweetened, a bit strong, or weak? Swirl it around in your mouth to fully open up your taste buds. Consciously and subconsciously use all your senses together to obtain information. It makes a big difference in your perceptions of something as ordinary and everyday as a glass of iced tea.

With these exercises, you became more in tune with and aware of the energy vibrations of *everyday* items, feelings, memories, images, and events. As you fully develop your physical senses, you can use them in many more ways than to sense and be completely aware of things on a conscious, physical level. Increased physical awareness is a prelude to opening up your natural psychic and spiritual perceptions and using them in connection with your physical senses to see, hear, feel, smell, and taste with your mind.

MIND-POWER EXERCISES

Now that you know how to revitalize and enhance your physical senses, use them in your day-to-day activities to sense the situations you're in and the things you're experiencing in a fully aware, focused manner—with all your senses functioning together. Consciously become aware of things that previously escaped your attention because they seemed to be so ordinary. Sense everything completely with your body, your mind, and your emotions. Experience the things in life as the truly magical, special things they really are.

You'll notice how much more vibrant and alive your experiences are and how much more aware of everything you are. This may start out very subtly, but the more you involve your senses every day, with every experience you have and with everything you do, the more you'll become aware of and the clearer your impressions will be. As a fringe benefit, you'll also find that your memory will improve dramatically.

CHAPTER NINE

Psychic Senses

Your sixth sense is psychic awareness—your sense of inner knowing and understanding with your mind the vibrations of everything in your life, both within and outside of yourself. You've probably heard the term ESP, which means extra sensory perception. It's a catch-all phrase for abilities relating to psychic awareness. I take exception to this term because it implies that your psychic abilities are extra—that they're unnatural and separate from you and out of harmony with your physical senses. Not so. You were born with all your psychic abilities perfectly intact and functioning on a completely aware level, just like your five physical senses. Your psychic senses may have been largely ignored to the point where they've now become dormant, or previous programming might have squelched them or tried to put them out of your reach by stating that they belonged to gifted people.

The only difference between people who are psychic and those who think they aren't is the time that a person takes to redevelop their natural psychic abilities. Everyone already has true knowledge and awareness within themselves. Psychic awareness surfaces easily in a positive person. Let's change that term and correctly refer to **all** your sensory perceptions as *extra special*. Put your psychic abilities in their rightful place—in the power of your own mind.

By the way, you have more than six senses. You have seven. Your seventh sense is spiritual awareness; it's your sense of spiritual knowledge and your awareness of your true spiritual nature. As you go within yourself, you completely open up and redevelop your natural abilities of psychic perception, and you tune into the magical, mystical power of your mind.

You use your psychic awareness every day without consciously thinking about it. Whenever you have a *hunch* or a *feeling* or a sense of knowing something without knowing how you know, you're using your psychic abilities instinctively. The dictionary defines *instinct* as "an inborn tendency to behave in a natural, unacquired mode of response; innate." *Innate* is defined as "possessed at birth; inborn; intrinsic, existing naturally, rather than acquired." *Intrinsic* is defined as "within, belonging to the real nature; inherent." *Inherent* is defined as "existing in someone as a natural and inseparable quality, characteristic or right; innate, basic, inborn." *Inborn* is defined as "present at birth; innate; natural; not acquired." Psychic abilities are natural, and they're your spiritual birthright! Note that all these definitions begin with the prefix *in*, meaning inner or within.

Speaking of inner, let's look at *insight*, which is defined as "the ability to see and understand clearly the inner nature of things, especially by intuition." *Intuition* is defined as "the direct knowing of something without the conscious use of reasoning, immediate understanding, the ability to perceive or know things without conscious reasoning." You use intuition—your sense of inner knowing— to obtain information about every situation you find yourself in. The more you listen to your inner self and tune into your feelings, the more you'll become aware of on an intuitive level. Intuition is interrelated with telepathy and precognition.

Telepathy is defined as "communication between minds; transference of thought." Telepathy is the ability to read another person's thoughts, to know what's on their mind, and to transmit your thoughts, images, and impressions. You've probably had the experience of knowing what someone was going to say before he or she said it, or maybe you've both said the same thing at the same time. Or maybe someone spoke the thoughts you had in your mind or you discovered that you were thinking the same thing.

If someone is thinking about you, his or her thoughts and feelings, being composed of energy, are transmitted to you and received by you on a subconscious level. You also send signals—waves of energy—to everyone and everything around you, without consciously being aware of doing this. People respond unconsciously to thought energy. Maybe you've thought of someone you haven't seen for a while and the next day he or she called you or you ran into him or her, seemingly by chance or an amazing coincidence.

Telepathy operates on thought energy. This ability is a two-way street—sending and receiving. Telepathy is like tuning into frequencies of energy—like tuning into radio waves. It depends on what channel you're tuned into as to what information you become aware of. Your mind operates on a current of energy similar to radio waves. When you select the channel, by your thoughts, and you flip the switch, by your feelings, you turn on the power and the waves of energy are available to you on a conscious level.

In the same way that you send and receive thought energies, you also become aware of situations that haven't happened yet or of things that will happen in a situation that's in progress. *Precognition* is defined as "previous knowing or awareness; perception of an event, condition, etc., before it occurs." While you may already know certain things about what has happened in a situation and what is probably going to occur based on your expectations as well as some good old-fashioned common sense, precognition and intuition can provide you with some interesting and unexpected information.

Very often, precognition occurs out of the clear blue sky, and you just suddenly become aware of something that's going to happen that's unrelated to anything else that is going on in your life at the moment. For example, three months before my daughter was conceived, I knew that I would be having another child—a girl. This information came to me as I was sitting in my kitchen eating pizza and thinking about the wallpaper I was going to put up.

You pick up precognitive information in several ways—through your thoughts and inner images, on an intuitive or a *feeling* level, through a dream, and even through *déjà vu*—which is a sense of familiarity, of having seen something or of having been somewhere before. This brings up an interesting idea that perhaps déjà vu is more than it appears to be. Maybe your mind projected into the future and saw what was going to happen, and then the information—which you've previously become aware of or already experienced but have now forgotten on a conscious level—pops into your mind when you're least expecting it.

A *premonition* is similar to precognition; it's a feeling that something bad is going to happen. It's easy to mistake a fear or a worry as a premonition. By seeing it for what it is and by working with what is in your control to change, very often you can prevent potential fears from turning into physical situations. If you become aware of a premonition when you're feeling negative or depressed,

look to the possibility that it could be an outgrowth of
your negative feelings and not a premonition.

Intuition and precognitive information give you both the
power and the foresight to change or prevent events before
they happen. You can shape the possibilities and restruc-
ture the probabilities of future situations based on what
you do now. This is especially helpful in the case of a premonition. If the event relates only to you, more than likely
you'll be able to change it—if you choose to. If someone
else is involved, you may or may not be able to change all
of it, but you can certainly change the part you play in it.
Perhaps you could choose not to participate in the upcom-
ing event or not to place yourself in the wrong place at
the wrong time. The way you work with your thoughts
and feelings, and with the energies of the unmanifested situation, will determine its outcome.

Your psychic perceptions don't need to be earth-shat-
tering to get your attention. They may relate to seemingly
small and insignificant things, but when you follow your
feelings, it makes a big difference! One day, for no apparent reason, I had a feeling to unplug my television. I was
in a rush to get to work, but I took the time to do it. When
I got home that evening, I discovered that my dog had
chewed through the cord. If I'd left the TV plugged in, my
dog would have been electrocuted.

Another time I didn't follow my feelings because they
weren't very strong and there didn't appear to be any specific reason for them. I had a feeling to go outside to
check on my daughter, who was seven years old at the

time. She was playing nearby with her friends and I looked out the window and saw that she was safe. I didn't go, and a few minutes later she came in crying. She had found a caterpillar and made friends with it. When she showed it to one of the little boys, he smashed it. If I'd followed my feelings and gone outside, maybe that wouldn't have happened. It was just a small feeling that I ignored, but it would have made a big difference to my daughter (and to the caterpillar).

Another time I was about to turn left on a yellow light. The light changed to red, and while I could have made the turn easily, I had a feeling not to. I waited till the light changed to green, and after I turned I saw a police car that had been hidden from view, sitting on a side street just waiting for unsuspecting motorists. If I'd turned, I would have gotten a ticket.

While it's gratifying to see results when you follow your feelings and act on your psychic perceptions, very often nothing appears to have been changed; however, you've altered the energies of situations and you have changed things, sometimes very dramatically.

Be open and receptive to what comes to you psychically. You don't need to understand something consciously in order to know that it's right and to act on it. Pay attention to your feelings and accept them. Listen to yourself, to your inner voice; don't doubt, dissect, and destroy on a conscious level what you become aware of. Psychic information may seem to make no sense and may appear to be out of context. This is because your psychic senses operate on a subconscious level, and conscious characteristics such as time, space, logic, and reason don't apply. It's important to follow your inner feelings and to trust your instincts.

It goes without saying that the more you use your psychic senses on a daily basis, the more you'll fully develop them, be able to put them together with your conscious mind and your physical senses, and fine-tune them to peak perfection, where they'll blend easily into all your everyday activities to enhance everything you do.

MIND-POWER EXERCISES

The following exercises are suggestions to help you open up and increase your psychic perceptions. You might want to keep an ongoing journal of all the instances where you've become aware of psychic information or used your psychic abilities. Include your insights and intuitive feelings, your precognitive perceptions, and the telepathic thoughts and images you send and receive. This will show you how often you use your psychic awareness every day; it's a lot more than you might think.

1. Define and describe what being psychic means to you. This will help you understand what you want to achieve by increasing your psychic awareness. Make a list of all the ways you can use and allow your natural psychic abilities to help you on a day-to-day, practical level.

2. Think about phone calls you'll be receiving—who the caller is and what they'll say. Think about mail you'll be receiving—who it's from and what the contents are. Picture what the envelopes will look like—their size and color. Think about people you'll see during the day—what they'll be wearing and what they'll say or do.

3. Picture your best friend with your mind's eye. Telepathically ask him or her to call you at a certain time. When this is successful, transmit a thought to someone you're not close to, such as an acquaintance, requesting that they call you on a specific day. Make sure this person has your phone number. (Soon you won't need a telephone any more. You can just communicate with your mind.)

4. Work with a friend to increase your telepathic abilities. You already have a strong sense of telepathy with people you're close to because you have a natural rapport with them. At a prearranged time, tune into the vibrations of your friend's thoughts, feelings, images, and impressions of a picture or another object that he or she is looking at, or a place that he or she is in. Write down all the information you become aware of. Later, compare notes with your friend to see the similarities between what you received and what your friend was sending. Then, switch roles. You be the sender and see what your friend picks up.

This is also known as remote perception and can help you tune into situations that are occurring outside of your physical proximity. I use this when my teenage daughters are late coming home to find out if they're OK and where they are. I picture them in my mind, tune into their energy vibrations and look around them to see their surroundings. This works wonderfully well if I haven't allowed worry to get in my way. (Note: Use this ability wisely. It's not nice to spy. Make sure your intentions are pure and positive and that you have a right to know this information. Respect a person's right to privacy.)

5. Develop your own Mind-Power Exercises based on what you want to explore and what is important to you. Work with your psychic awareness in the way that feels right for you. Note which abilities are stronger and which ones you feel most in tune with. Record all the details, your feelings, and the results.

6. Every once in a while, review how your psychic abilities of intuition, telepathy, and precognition are progressing. Reread your journal to see how they opened up and how you've redeveloped and allowed your abilities to flourish and grow. By using your natural psychic abilities on a daily basis, you'll hone them to perfection.

CHAPTER TEN

Discovering and Deciphering Your Dreams

Dreams are the bridge between your conscious and your subconscious awareness. They're more than just mind meanderings or a mirror image that reflects your feelings, thoughts, ideas, and experiences. Dreams are a magical and mystical doorway into your true spiritual nature and your inner knowledge. Inside your dreams, you have access to everything you've always wanted to know, and more. Your dreams can help you in every avenue of your life, and you can do anything you want to do with your dreams.

Dreams are very special; they're a wonderful and powerful resource of your subconscious mind that you have available to you every night. Dream studies have shown that you spend approximately one to one-and-a-half hours dreaming four or five dreams every night. Your dreams are unique; they're as individual as you are. There are many types of dreams that show you various things about yourself and your life, and they cover all areas and every level of awareness. The partial list that follows barely scratches the surface of the different types of dreams there are, but it gives you a general idea of what your dreams offer you and can help you identify and categorize your dreams to see the central theme.

ADVICE/ANSWER/INSIGHT. These dreams offer you insights, advice, or answers to something you've been wondering about or puzzling over. They can clearly explain things that you don't understand. This type of dream has sometimes been preceded by serious soul-searching and a concentrated conscious effort to figure something out.

ASTRAL PROJECTION. These aren't really dreams; they're out-of-body experiences that portray what your astral body is experiencing in its nightly sojourn. When you have dreams about floating or flying or falling, these can be astral projections where your astral body is leaving your physical body, traveling on an astral level, or returning to your body. If you become lucid during these experiences, you can consciously be aware of what your astral self is doing during these excursions. You astral project several times each night while you're in the deeper levels of sleep.

CONSCIOUS CONFLICT. These dreams are similar to problem-solving dreams, except they go one step further by making you aware of inner conflicts that you may not yet be aware of on a conscious level. These dreams are sometimes difficult to recall because you're not consciously dealing with the conflict for any variety of reasons. Your subconscious mind always strives to help you in the most positive and creative way it can by either showing you how to understand and resolve the conflict or by working through the conflict for you.

CONTINUING. This type of dream usually reflects ongoing situations that are happening in your life. They're like reading a book, chapter by chapter. As the dreams continue over a period of time, they may change and become lucid dreams or they may turn into precognitive dreams by showing you scenes that may occur in the future.

DAYDREAMS/FANTASIES/REVERIES. Daydreams are more than wishful thinking; they're a magical way into your mind. They spark creative ideas and endeavors. They offer you valuable insights and information into and about your experiences, and reveal your true feelings regarding the situation or person you're daydreaming about. They also help you to consciously create your own reality.

Daydreams are easy to remember and understand. The best way to decipher them is to look at the theme or outcome of the daydream. See what feelings play out and the purpose(s) it serves for you on an emotional level. Notice the situation you picture yourself in and how other people relate to you.

EVERYDAY, RUN-OF-THE-MILL. These dreams reflect what is occurring in your life right now that you're probably already aware of. They echo neutral events of the day and any books you may have read or movies or TV shows you may have seen recently. These dreams have special significance for you by highlighting your thoughts and feelings, or events that may have escaped your conscious attention during the day yet contain information you need to be aware of to function on an increased level of perception in your day-to-day activities. These dreams are usually literal, but they can sometimes be disguised or confusing because of the symbols you create to mirror the events in your life.

FEAR. These dreams replay fears, worries, and anxieties. They show you how you perceive and react to your fear. The content of these dreams may be difficult to recall, depending on where you're at in relation to understanding and working through your fear. They're usually symbolic and you tend to awaken immediately from the fear in the dream. If you remain asleep, these dreams will help you understand where your fear or worry originates and offer you ways to face and overcome your fear inside the dream.

One of my students was in the process of buying a house and was experiencing a lot of anxiety about it; he wasn't sure if he really wanted it or could afford it. In a dream, he saw himself walking into a half-finished house with his shirt off. He interpreted the dream to mean that if he bought the house, he would lose his shirt. He withdrew his offer. Several months later, he was transferred with his job to another state and found the perfect house that was within his price range.

FRIENDS/FAMILY. These dreams are similar to Psychic/Telepathic dreams and give you information about your friends and family, and what they're doing or are involved in. These dreams can also help you in your relationships or show you ways to help the people you care most about. When two people are closely connected with one another, they'll often dream the same dream or participate in each other's dream.

GOAL-ORIENTED. These dreams offer you a clear direction for setting and achieving goals that you're beginning to think about. They show you what you need to do and make you aware of stepping stones that lead to success. They're often a prelude to how-to-do-it dreams.

HEALTH/HEALING. These dreams serve a dual purpose. They warn you of impending health problems and offer you avenues to pursue that will prevent the potential illness or dis-ease from manifesting. They help you understand the symbology of your symptoms and show you how to keep your physical body healthy by letting you know what to do for yourself. If you've already established a health problem, they may advise you to see a doctor or offer you alternative or holistic methods of creating the cure. They sometimes suggest natural remedies that are easily obtainable. One of my dreams told me to eat peaches to effectuate a healing for a problem that was beginning

to manifest. I ate the peaches and was better within a
week.

These dreams also may instruct you to change your way
of thinking or feeling about certain events or people. Sometimes a cure consists of changing something in your life,
like changing a job or letting go of a relationship that is
causing you a lot of stress, or just simply changing your
perceptions about it.

Very often, doctors or nurses appear in health dreams.
One of my students was experiencing an ongoing health
problem. Over a period of time, she dreamed about a Chi-
nese doctor who gave her a bit of metaphysical/oriental
philosophy. As she applied the philosophy in her life, the
doctor offered her herbal teas and acupuncture treatments
in her sleep. The teas and treatment, along with the philosophy, healed her.

How-TO-DO-IT. These dreams offer specific instructions
by showing you the best way for you to accomplish whatever it is that you want to achieve. They're similar to goal-
oriented and inspiration dreams. They're usually quite
literal and give you a detailed, step-by-step plan. They tell
you exactly what to do, how to do it, and when. They may
also tell you why you want and need to do it, and if anyone else is involved and the part they play. They help you
turn a dream into a reality.

IDEA/INSPIRATION. These dreams offer you inspiration
by opening up your intuition and creativity. They may

show you a single image or a clear, simple scene. This type of dream seems to sparkle with light and often gives you ideas or a new thought perspective. When you follow the guidance given in your dreams, your ideas and thoughts spill over from your subconscious and begin to flow on a conscious, physical level.

LEARNING/TEACHING. These dreams help you learn things that you want to know by teaching you on many levels. On a spiritual level, they're similar to astral projections and can help to put you in touch with your true spiritual nature. This type of dream opens up your full awareness and gives you access to your inner, spiritual knowledge. During the dream, you may be aware of your higher self or of spirit guides and masters who are teaching and guiding you. This type of dream also helps you learn life lessons and shows you the spiritual purposes you've set out to accomplish in this lifetime.

On a physical level these dreams learn things for you that you don't have time to devote your full attention to during the day. One of my students had to learn a new software program at work in a very short time. She pored over the manual by day and learned the computer codes and their applications by night.

LUCID. These are dreams during which you're awake at the same time you're asleep. Supposedly this is impossible, but it happens all the time. This type of dream is one of the best examples of how your subconscious bridges the

span between physical and psychic/spiritual awareness.
Inside the dream, you're consciously aware that you're
dreaming.

You can do whatever you want to do with lucid dreams.
One of my students uses them as a takeoff point for astral
projections. Other students direct the dream and create
any outcome they want as they continue to sleep and
dream. These dreams show you that you're in control of
the circumstances and situations in your life, and show you
how you create your own reality.

Lucid dreams make you wonder how real your dreams
truly are. It's been said that we dream everything before
it happens. What if your life is just a dream you're having? I wonder . . . ?

MESSAGE. These dreams give you messages of a physical, psychic, or spiritual nature that are important for you
to consciously be aware of. They're usually about a major
event or a big change that you or someone very close to
you will be experiencing in the near future. They're set in
the present time and the scene is usually in your home.
Most often, friends or relatives who have died appear in
the dream to give you the message. The dreams are usually very brief and quite literal, and there's a loving quality associated with them. You wake up with a feeling of
being cared about and cared for, and you wonder if you
dreamed it or if it really happened.

NIGHTMARES. These dreams are screaming for your
attention. They're usually shrouded in symbology, but the

content in them is something you need to be made aware of. That's why you can always remember them, because they wake you up in the middle of the night and really make you think!

You can dream about fearful or unpleasant things in a happy, positive way. One of my students said that when she was a little girl, she'd have nightmares every night and wake up screaming in terror. One night she decided to say a little prayer before she went to sleep. She prayed that she would only dream about happy things. She's never had a nightmare since.

PAST LIVES/REINCARNATION. These dreams replay important events and emotions that you experienced in previous lives that are currently affecting you. Whatever these dreams portray is something you've carried over to this lifetime that needs to be worked on to achieve balance and understanding. These dreams may recur until you've worked through your karma. This type of dream helps you to further evolve your soul.

PRECOGNITIVE. These dreams allow you to travel through time to see into and experience the future. They tell you of an occurrence that will happen and offer you insights into your part in the event(s) to come. These events may relate to you specifically or they may involve other people. The dreams give you the opportunity to change things now in your life if you choose to, thereby changing the energies and expressions of future experiences.

PREMONITION/WARNING. These dreams are similar to precognitive dreams except you wake up with a vague sense of foreboding or a definite feeling of dread, depending on the nature of the future event. They warn you of dangers, usually of a significant nature, that may occur. These dangers could be physical dangers or a warning to beware of particular people or actions you're taking in your life.

For example, if you were to dream about a pillow being shredded and you saw the white stuffing flying all around, what would that mean to you? Suppose it was the middle of winter when you dreamed this and you had a car trip planned for the next day. Depending on your feelings and what else was in the dream, it could be warning you to either cancel your trip or to be careful driving because of the snow.

PROBLEM-SOLVING. These dreams solve your problems for you. They offer you solutions and show you the best way of working through any problem you have and bringing it to a perfect resolution. (More on this later.)

PSYCHIC/TELEPATHIC. You're naturally psychic when you're dreaming because you're completely tuned into your subconscious mind. These dreams offer you insights and information about people and events in your life. They can also relay messages from other people. Telepathy occurs frequently in dreams.

When you have a dream about someone you know, share your dream with them. It may help them in something they're thinking about or experiencing. It may help them to reach a decision or give them valuable insights. One night I dreamed about a student and a shoe box hidden in her closet. The next night in class, I told her about the dream. She said she'd been searching everywhere for some important papers. When she went home that evening, she found the shoe box exactly where I'd seen it in my dream. The missing papers were inside.

RECURRING. These dreams replay the same theme over and over again, sometimes in slightly different versions, to give you important information or to help you see things that are buried deeply in your subconscious mind. Sometimes they're symbolic because they can replay traumatic experiences or fears. They also occur when your subconscious wants to get your attention to make you aware of specific matters. They can help you work through longstanding problems or fears that take time to resolve. These dreams will continue until you accurately interpret what they're telling you and do something about it.

REMINDER. These dreams remind you of something you have to do that you've pushed to the back of your mind and forgotten about on a conscious level. One of my students made an appointment to see the dentist but didn't mark it on his calendar. The night before his appointment, he had a dream about a giant tooth pursuing him.

STAR (PRAISE, APPROVAL, AND SELF-APPRECIATION). These dreams are your subconscious's way of telling you that you're a really special person. They occur to congratulate you when you've accomplished something that's important to you or when you've made a dream come true. They also occur when you don't take the time to appreciate yourself on a conscious level. It's a nice way for your subconscious to show you that you're appreciated and that your efforts are recognized.

Dreams don't happen by chance. They occur for many reasons and can be influenced by what's on your mind and what's going on in your life. Your thoughts and feelings prior to going to sleep will go directly into your subconscious and will influence your dreams and the quality of your sleep. Going to sleep naturally and peacefully, with positive thoughts on your mind, ensures a good night's sleep and can help you remember your dreams. You can give yourself positive presleep suggestions. Tell yourself, "I'm going to enjoy a peaceful, healthy night's sleep. I'll wake up in the morning feeling refreshed and full of energy, with a clear and vivid recollection of my dreams. I'll be able to understand and interpret them accurately."

In addition to helping you remember your dreams, this suggestion allows your mind to adjust itself during the night to the levels of sleep and dreaming that are necessary for your well-being. For instance, if you're only going to get four or five hours of sleep, your subconscious will automatically adjust itself to the deeper levels of mind while you sleep because this is where you're most refreshed and replenished.

The state of your mind and body upon awakening is meant to be calm and relaxed, not suddenly jarred into wakefulness by the sound of an alarm clock, or by hearing loud music or an announcer's voice on a clock radio intruding into your subconscious. I'm sure you know from experience that when you're roused abruptly from sleep, you feel disoriented and out of sync with yourself, and it takes a few minutes or longer before you're able to function effectively in a conscious, physical level.

You can wake up gently and naturally by adding some visualization into your presleep suggestions. Picture the clock in your bedroom at the time you want to wake up and tell yourself, "I'll wake up at this time feeling refreshed and full of energy."

Waking up at a specific time, with only the use of your mind, is something very easy to accomplish. You've probably done it many times before. It shows you how magical and powerful your mind is because it brings up an interesting question. *When you're asleep, how do you know what time it is?*

When you wake up gradually and gently, you go naturally from your subconscious into a conscious level. By waking up in a relaxed frame of mind, you're also setting the tone of your day to be pleasant and positive as well as more easily remembering and understanding your dreams.

Your dreams can help you do many magical and wonderful things with your mind. Keep a dream journal. Have a notebook and a pencil by your bed; when you wake up, write down everything you remember.

Usually the easiest dream to remember is the one you have just prior to waking up. Most people remember their dreams first thing in the morning, but it might be more convenient for you to remember them later that same day. Find the best time for you to remember your dreams and make it part of your daily routine.

Every dream contains important meanings for you. When you're first beginning to remember your dreams, it may seem like you're chasing elusive images, or putting the pieces of a puzzle together and most of the pieces seem to be missing. Your dreams may be fragmented, or you may remember only one or two things. You may recall a feeling about the dream without recalling the dream itself. Describe that feeling; very often it will trigger more about the dream. Your memory will improve each time you remember your dreams, and you'll soon be able to recall every detail in all your dreams.

As you keep a written record of them, you'll find that your dreams will help you in understanding yourself and your experiences on many levels of awareness, as well as reawakening you to your true spiritual nature. Include the following items in your dream journal:

1. The date you had the dream
2. The dream; note your initial impression and first feelings about it

3. What type of dream it was (the central theme or main message)
4. Your thoughts and feelings just prior to falling asleep (include presleep suggestions and dream programming)
5. The events of the last few days and your plans for the next few days (these may be interwoven in your dreams)
6. Your dream imagery—symbols that seem especially significant and what they represent to you
7. Your in-depth interpretation of the dream, and how the dream affects or impacts your life
8. Any other information that you feel is important

Deciphering your dreams is easy once you understand and apply a few basic principles of the process of dreaming. Your conscious self and your dreaming self are as different as night and day. When you dream, you open up your subconscious mind to its full expression. Your subconscious communicates through imagery and symbolism, and your conscious perceptions have little value in your dream world.

Some dreams are literal and interpret themselves for you. Others may contain symbols drawn by your subconscious mind that portray revealing pictures about your true feelings and the events and people and circumstances in your life. Look at the overall content and context of the dream. Note the events in the dream and their relationship to the dream. Pay attention to even the smallest details; every detail can prove to be significant.

There are many dream-interpretation books that will tell you what your subconscious is saying to you, but I prefer to read my own mind. You write your own dream imagery based on your experiences, your frame of reference and on your inner knowledge. It's also based on what you've heard about, what you've read, what other people have told you, how you were brought up, and on your thoughts, feelings, and perceptions about everything in your life.

BUT, and this is a big but, if you've read a book on dream interpretation and you believe that a certain symbol represents something, and then you dream about that symbol, that symbol will represent what you believe it to represent.

Everyone has their own personal dream symbols. For example, I don't know what a chicken is supposed to represent in a dream book, but the chicken walking around making noises in one of my dreams showed me something that I was afraid to do. Later in that same dream, when the chicken was in a sandwich, it meant that I had overcome my fear.

And I don't know what a dream-interpretation book would tell me about a bunny rabbit with red eyes named Carroll, but I know that the rabbit who appeared in one of my dreams—as I was lost and wandering through time and reflections of mirror images—represented a kahuna (Hawaiian shaman) who offered to be my guide. (I read

Alice's Adventures in Wonderland and *Through the Looking-Glass* by Lewis Carroll when I was a child. I've been doing shamanic journeying for several years, and on this trip, I needed help to explore a particular area.)

You're the only one who can accurately translate your subconscious symbolism into words. Decipher your dream symbols based on your feelings about the symbol and what it represents to you. If you're unclear about a symbol's meaning, do a reverie and ask the symbol what it represents. Listen to your feelings or look for an image to get the answer. You can also switch roles with the symbol. Question the symbol, then become the symbol and answer from the symbol's point of view. Another way to understand your dream symbols is to use free association. Think of the symbol, then note all the related perceptions and feelings you have about it. Another good way to decipher the symbol is to use a presleep suggestion to tell your subconscious to have a dream that will explain the symbol to you.

It's been said that a picture is worth a thousand words. As you interpret your dream, you translate and transform the images into words that show the meanings of your dreams. If you try to analyze your dreams in a conscious level, you'll lose most, if not all, of the true meaning in the transition from your subconscious to your conscious mind. Interpret your dreams in the same way they were presented to you—in your subconscious mind. Gently ponder your dreams and your feelings about them to see what the symbols represent and what the dream shows you and says to you. When you accurately interpret a dream, you'll get a feeling that clicks in your mind that lets you know you've clearly understood your dream.

When you become adept at remembering and understanding your dreams, you can program them to do anything you want them to do! Many people use their dreams to help them solve problems without being aware that this is what they're doing. When they're faced with a problem or a decision they'll say, "I'll sleep on it," or "Things will be clearer in the morning."

You can generate a dream to solve a problem for you in a clear, conscious way. Tell yourself, "I want to have a dream that will solve this problem." State or view your problem thoroughly as it exists now, without dwelling on the negative aspects. Also, and this is very important, don't try to second-guess how your subconscious will solve the problem and don't offer possible solutions. If you do, your dreams will mirror those conscious thoughts. But, on the other hand, you may have just come up with the solution for yourself.

After stating the problem, say, "I'll have a dream that gives me the perfect solution to this problem. When I wake up in the morning, I'll clearly remember my dream and understand it easily." Then just go to sleep, naturally and peacefully, knowing that your subconscious already has and will give you the perfect solution. First thing in the morning, the dream will either pop into your mind or you'll become aware of the solution through a feeling or an image.

You can do so much more than solve problems in your sleep. Whatever you want your dreams to do, they will do. You can create any kind of dream you want. The way to program a specific type of dream is to simply tell your subconscious mind what you want it to do. That's all there is to it. You might want to think about what you're going to say to your subconscious before you're laying in bed, half asleep, so you can word your dream suggestions to be very powerful and effective.

MIND-POWER EXERCISES

Your dreams are a magical, mystical place to be. They aren't limited by the physical concepts of time, space, or matter. They're multidimensional and offer you access into other realms of reality and levels of awareness. Explore your dreams. See what's inside your mind.

CHAPTER ELEVEN

Creating Your Own Reality

Creating your own reality is like a magical, mystical game that you play with your mind. It's magical because it works with the power of your thoughts and feelings, and it's mystical because you're seeing and shaping invisible energies as you transform them into your experiences. There's only one rule; the rest of the rules are dictated, designed, and defined by you. The best part is that you can do whatever you want to do.

You already know how to create your own reality because you do it every day. Your experiences are a mirror of your thoughts. If you look carefully into and at your present experiences, you'll see how your previous thoughts, feelings, actions, beliefs, desires, and expectations created those experiences. You'll see how you played the game before and you'll see that you can choose to play it differently now.

If you want to change your experiences, you have to see things as they truly are. By acknowledging and accepting what **is** at this specific moment in time, you can create what **can be**. You can clearly and **consciously** create the reality you want to experience by recognizing that your thoughts are tangible things. Maybe not the moment you think them, but sooner or later your thoughts appear in your life in the form of experiences.

That's the rule. It's called *cause and effect*. Every thought you have is a *cause* that creates an *effect*. You cause events to happen and you attract people and situations into your life through your thoughts. Then you experience the results—the effects—of your previous thoughts, feelings, and actions.

The power of your thoughts is truly awesome. You create your reality from the inside out by working with the unseen energies of your thoughts and by playing with possibilities and probabilities inside your imagination. Your experiences are the energy expressions of your thoughts. The way you use your imagination determines what you experience; your attitude and expectations determine how you experience it. That's how the game is played.

But first a few words about beliefs, because that's where the game begins and ends. Your beliefs form your thoughts and feelings, which create your experiences; then your experiences reflect and reinforce your beliefs. If you want to change your reality, change your beliefs, which will then change your thoughts and feelings. That's what self-empowerment and accepting responsibility for your reality is all about—knowing that you have the magical power to change your reality, to make it whatever you want it to be.

Speaking of magic, this is where your inner power comes into full play, and where you can clearly and consciously create your own reality through your imagination. You will bring into your life whatever you envision in the way that you perceive it and believe it. That's why it's so important to know what your beliefs are and to have a positive attitude. When you're working with your thoughts, you're working with invisible energy. The way you shape and mold that energy inside your mind—your imagination—will turn out to be the way that energy becomes visible in your experiences.

Working with invisible energies is not mysterious or mind-boggling. It's actually quite simple. Here's an example of how it works in three easy steps: One—I think about writing a book. That thought exists as invisible energy. Two—As I work with that energy and write the book, it begins to come to life—to exist in my physical reality. Three—You're holding the physical (tangible) manifestation of my invisible thought in your hands.

There are many things to keep in mind as you create your reality. Let's look at the misperception that limits are negative. Limits are positive when they clearly define the scope of what you want to create in your reality. For example, by deciding the main theme or topic of my book, I've set limits that clearly define the scope of what I want my book to say.

For another example: You decide to create a wonderful career for yourself. By deciding what you want your career to be, you've set limits. This allows you to clearly define and direct your thoughts. Otherwise you'd be saying, "I want a wonderful career," but you wouldn't be able to harness and direct the correct energies to manifest what you want. Limits are a way of concentrating and focusing energies to achieve your desires. But watch how you work with limits; they can be a little tricky. Keep your mind open for ideas and images to flow and be willing to change your mind and rearrange your thoughts.

This brings us back to beliefs again. You have to believe that this career is possible and that it's going to happen. Then through your imagination, you shape it into a real probability. With the power of your mind, you determine how and when it will happen through your thoughts and feelings and through the ideas and insights you become aware of and see in your imagination. Then you make it happen by following through with actions. Even if you just sit back and wait for it to happen, your wonderful career will still manifest in direct proportion to the energy you give it. *Once you create a thought, that thought will turn into a tangible thing.*

An important consideration in reality creation is where your reality touches other people. When your reality involves someone else, make it clear in your mind that your desired reality is for the best for all concerned. There's a fringe benefit to this; it will very often bring about something even better than you first envisioned.

Creating your own reality brings a lot of elements into play, including setting time frames, having realistic and reasonable expectations, being flexible and going with the flow, looking into the past and seeing into the future while being completely in the present, shaping and sculpting energies, focusing and directing your thoughts and images, being clear and specific, knowing your heart's desires, changing your mind, building power through secrecy and generating energy through wishes, releasing requests, receiving help from higher sources, listening to yourself, taking risks and totally trusting, following your feelings, becoming aware of alternate avenues to pursue, and maybe falling over a few stumbling blocks before you recognize that they're stepping stones to success.

I could describe in detail how to create your reality (what to expect, things to watch out for, what to do, how it all works, and stuff like that) but that would be cheating you out of the most fun part of the game—the joy of discovering for yourself how **you** create **your** reality. Besides, everything I could say would reflect my perceptions and philosophies of what *I* believe about reality. And

I think you've opened up the magical power of your mind and you're self-empowered to find the truth for yourself.

So I'm going to do what any real teacher would do. I'm going to let you learn for yourself through your experiences, because they're your best teacher. But I will give you a word of warning and one helpful hint. You'll get what you think you deserve, not necessarily what you think you want. This usually turns out to be very interesting for you. And if you have a good sense of humor, it can also be quite entertaining. The most important part of creating your own reality—a positive, beautiful, wonderful, magical, mystical reality—is to know that you create everything that happens in your life for a special reason to help you in a beneficial way. Look inside your experiences to see that special reason.

MIND-POWER EXERCISES

1. Take an honest look at your reality—at the experiences, both good and bad—that you've created and allowed into your life. Then ask yourself what you were thinking before these experiences occurred. This will give you a clear idea of what your beliefs are and will show you how to change them if you choose. It's easy to know what your beliefs are because your experiences clearly show you what you believe. Look into the situations that continually repeat themselves in slightly different versions and you'll see what your main beliefs are. This will also help you see how your thoughts and feelings shape your experiences and how you've played the game so far.

If you have trouble recognizing your beliefs, pretend that your reality is happening to someone else. Look at their reality to see what they were thinking and what their beliefs must be in order for them to have created what they're experiencing. This can give you wonderful insights and help you see inside your own thoughts.

2. Think about your most recent accomplishment or one that is very special to you. Notice how and when the thought of it first presented itself and the ideas, information, insights, and images that played in your imagination. Look at all the actions you took to achieve your goal, the events and opportunities that occurred along the way, and what you did about them. Remember how you felt when you achieved your goal and why you felt the way you did. This will show you, step-by-step, how you create your own reality.

3. Define, in detail, what being happy means to you. Then write a list of things that make you happy. Go through this list and write the reasons these things make you happy. Make a second list of things that you thought would make you happy but didn't. Describe how and why they made you unhappy.

Make another list of things you want now that would make you happy. Go through this list and clearly describe

why these things would make you happy. Your definition
of happiness and these three lists will help you become
clear and specific about what you want to create and experience in your reality and why you want it. They'll also
help you get in touch with your true feelings and show
you where to focus and direct your thoughts to achieve
happiness.

4. Be appreciative of the reality you've created that you're
now experiencing. See all the good in it. The benefits of
doing this will become obvious to you.

5. Recall an experience where you wanted a situation to
manifest that might have seemed impossible at first. Think
back to the events that occurred and see if you can pin-
point help from higher sources, such as ideas and insights
that popped into your mind out of a clear blue sky, or
events and chances and coincidences that you never considered or put into the picture. This will show you how
positive universal energies come into play, and how they
operate when you believe that everything will work out
perfectly and you'll get what you want, even if you haven't
got a clue about how to proceed.

There are some special fringe benefits to this exercise.
You may become even more aware of your higher self—
the keeper of all your knowledge—or perhaps you'll meet
a spiritual master or your guardian angel. You'll see the
mystical power you have within you because when you

open up the magic of your mind, you open up the mystical vibrations of your spiritual nature and allow yourself to experience the higher energies of your soul and the universe.

6. Create your own reality in a clear, conscious way. Generate lots of positive energy every day, in everything you think, say, and do. Then watch your thoughts turn into tangible things.

CHAPTER TWELVE

Health and Harmony

You have the power to experience and enjoy perfect health in body, mind, and spirit. Your body wants to be healthy and always strives for harmony with your beliefs, thoughts, and feelings.

If I were to ask you if you've ever abused yourself or beaten yourself up, you'd probably say no—but I'd have to disagree with you. Any negative thought or emotion that you have and hold literally beats up your body, which responds by becoming hurt and crying out for help. Your body experiences *dis-ease* with your negative thoughts, feelings, and beliefs. Your body expresses this negativity in your experiences, sometimes in the form of sickness, in order to bring you back to balance and health. This is a very positive thing and shows how your body, working in harmony with your mind, does its best to take care of you.

A good example of this is the common cold, for which there is no cure because the cold itself is the cure. It places your body in a healing environment, even though you appear to be sick, and allows you to get rid of negative, clogged up thoughts and emotions. There's nothing quite like a good sneeze to clear your mind, not to mention your sinuses.

The power of your thoughts and feelings can either keep you healthy or make you sick. You're sometimes your own worst enemy—albeit unconsciously—in preventing yourself from enjoying perfect health. Any type of dis-ease is a lack of positive energy flowing in that area. When you experience sickness, the dis-ease shows you that you're out of tune with your spiritual nature and out of balance with the flow of positive energy. Your body knows how to take care of itself and will heal itself if you'll cooperate.

The symbology of sickness is very interesting and enlightening. Look into your life to see what you're say-ing to yourself. Your mind listens to and does exactly what you tell it to do. Look at the way your dis-ease is expressed to know what thoughts and feelings you're putting into your subconscious mind. You make yourself sick in a way that symbolizes exactly what you need to do to get better. Your body will show you what's wrong and tell you how to make it right. When you look at the way the sickness is expressed, you know what you're doing to yourself and what you believe.

For example, take a look at back pain. Suppose you're in a situation that you feel is too much to take care of or one that you'd rather not deal with, so you say or think to yourself, "I can't stand this." You're telling yourself to experience back problems or muscle weakness in your legs. When you're ready to stand up for yourself—to take care of the situation in a positive manner—your back will get better.

It's within your power to be completely healthy. Just think positive thoughts and keep reminding yourself that you're perfectly healthy. If you want to make yourself sick, that's also within your power. Just let negative thoughts and feelings run rampant through your mind and keep telling yourself things like "This situation or person is a pain in the neck. This person gives me a headache. This is hard for me to say. I don't want to hear this." Etc., etc., etc.

Look into the above sentences: "This person gives me a headache." You're telling yourself to have a headache every time you see, or think about, or talk to this person. "This is hard for me to say." You're giving yourself a sore throat. "I don't want to hear this." You're giving yourself an earache. Shall I go on or have you heard enough?

If I were to ask you again if you've ever beaten yourself up, what would you say now? Wince, ouch, yes. Let go of your negative thoughts and feelings; they can only hurt you. To help you feel better, look into what you say and change your sick sentences into healthy statements that reflect your positive attitude.

Reality check: there are people and situations in your life that probably really are a pain in the neck (or worse), but you can keep yourself healthy by dealing with them in a positive way. Also keep your eyes open for the less obvious things that sneak up on you. Watch out for the way you respond to other people when they're telling you how sick they are or how badly they feel about something, or they're moaning about their problems.

Along those same lines, if you see yourself saying, thinking, or feeling something like "I feel helpless" or "This is hopeless," you may be giving your power away and falling into a self-induced trap of victim or martyr, or you may be allowing someone or something else to sap your energy and drain you of your positive attitude. Don't overlook accidents that happen to you. Accidents don't just happen; you create them on purpose for a specific reason so you can experience something.

Let's suppose that your negative thoughts and feelings have gotten the better of you. Health problems can be good learning experiences that you create for a variety of both positive and negative reasons. Maybe you create them to punish yourself for previous actions, to help you uncover or cover up your true feelings, or to appease guilt or another negative emotion. Maybe you create a sickness in response to unconscious or subconscious scripts, or to avoid taking responsibility for certain things. Sometimes a health problem can be a very beautiful life-changing experience—a way to help you learn a lesson or provide a way of accomplishing something or to show you how to turn tragedy into triumph. Perhaps you use an illness as a way to get attention or to get someone to do something for you, or because you feel you need the pain to push you in a certain direction. And sometimes you make yourself sick just so you can take a day off from work without feeling guilty about it.

Illness is your body's way of giving you messages, by showing and telling you what your thoughts and feelings are and what you need to do for yourself so you can experience health in body, mind, and spirit. Learn how to read your body. The aches and pains are talking to you, trying to tell you what is wrong that needs to be corrected. Your negative thoughts and feelings, whether they're conscious or unconscious, are the cause that precipitates the dis-ease, which is the effect. You can determine the cause by looking at the effect. This uncovers your underlying belief.

You can take care of the symptoms that show you the effect, but if the cause still exists, the dis-ease will recur until the cause is healed by changing your beliefs, thoughts, and feelings. Understand the cause and treat the cause. When you understand the message that underlies the outer expressions of sickness and dis-ease, you're well on the way to healing yourself.

You can heal yourself by becoming in tune with your positive nature and changing the way your thoughts and feelings express themselves. There isn't one particular way to do this that is better than another. Develop and design your own self-healing program. You already know, probably on a conscious level and definitely on an inner level, how to heal yourself and what will work best for you. Pay attention to your feelings and your intuition. Listen to your body; it will tell you what to do. Dreams will show you what to do. Your inner self will whisper healing ideas and your imagination will provide the images.

Visualization is a wonderful way to reestablish health. Once you have a health problem, you can either work from the inside out, finding the cause and curing it by changing the images of your thoughts and feelings, or you can work from the outside in, seeing the way the sickness is showing itself and changing those images to create perfect health in your body. Both ways work fine. (See Mind-Power Exercises #1 and #2.)

By the way, you don't need to be sick to use visualization to re-create health; you can use your inner imagery to appreciate everything your body does for you and to enjoy the perfect health you already have.

And, need I say it? It's always better to heal the hurt before it begins. Every once in a while, you might want to visualize your body to see images of potential health problems. The negativity usually shows up as a dark spot where the dis-ease is beginning to manifest. You can illuminate this dark spot with light to examine it closely and to see how you need to change your thoughts and feelings. Then surround and infuse the area with light to cleanse and fill it with healing energy. This is a very powerful and effective way of using white-light energy to heal yourself.

Whenever you're feeling a negative thought or emotion, bring it up to the surface and out into the open. Look at it in a loving, accepting, nonjudgmental way. Understand where it comes from and what caused it. Then turn the negative thought or emotion around to keep your positive thoughts and feelings in harmony with your body. You can do this in the same way that you turned fear into a friend or prevented a potential problem from manifesting.

Just as you sometimes unconsciously harm yourself, you also unconsciously heal yourself. Have you ever noticed that when you feel muscle stiffness or an ache or pain, an instinctive reaction is to massage the sore area? You're focusing and directing healing energy by increasing your circulation to the area of your body that needs it most, thus producing a feeling of warmth and comfort. Massaging the sore area allows energy to enter and begin the healing process. It's an acceptance and an acknowledgment of the pain, which is really a message that needs interpreting. It's also a message that you give to your body, saying, "I know you hurt, and I want you to feel better."

A precaution: with the power of your mind you can prevent pain and block symptoms, but this is not always a good idea. For example, what if you have a stomach ache and you eliminate the pain and misunderstand the message, and then three hours later your appendix ruptures? **Pain is a warning. Pay attention!**

Sometimes people allow themselves to become so sick that they need a doctor to help make them well. After the medical treatment—and after a person has changed their attitude and emotions—they become healthy. Sometimes, though, a complete cure won't come about, depending on the reasons why they created that experience and what they chose to learn from it. For example, a person may have a lifelong illness as a way to help themselves or others to grow and develop in many positive areas, or they may choose an incurable dis-ease as the way they want to die.

You have the power to heal yourself—to turn sickness into health. You're the only one who has that power, even if you allow a doctor or a treatment to help you. Healing occurs when you take full responsibility for your dis-ease, understand the negative message you've been giving yourself, and change that message on an inner level. You may obtain instantaneous results, or the healing process may take time. It depends on your beliefs, thoughts, and feelings. It may also be dependent on how long your negativity has been in place.

Your belief is what makes and keeps you healthy. Look at the power of the placebo. Placebos are sugar pills that have no medicinal value. They work simply because people believe they will work. There have been numerous scientific studies done that point out that belief is the healing factor.

In one study, two groups of people who suffered from migraine headaches were told that the medication they were receiving would alleviate their pain. The first group was given drugs. The second group was given placebos. The results showed that both groups reported relief from their headaches. The placebos were just as effective as the drugs, because the people taking them *believed* that the placebos were strong drugs that would cure their headaches.

A person's mind, based on his or her beliefs, causes his or her body to release endorphins that eliminate the pain and facilitate healing. Endorphins are the body's natural all-purpose painkillers and general all-around, feel-good, magical mind messengers of health and well-being.

Your body responds to your beliefs. When you believe that the self-healing program you've created for yourself and put into action, or the doctor you're seeing, or the treatment you're receiving, or the medicine you're taking will cure whatever is wrong with you, then it will. Believe that you're healthy and follow through with positive thoughts, feelings, and actions.

One of the best ways to be healthy is to be happy and smile a lot. Smiling does so much more than increase your sense of well-being and your positive attitude and self-image. You just plain feel good when you smile. In addition to making you happy, smiling will help to keep you healthy because smiling also releases endorphins.

Laughter has been proven to have tremendous value in healing. Sometimes you can cure yourself of the most dread dis-eases just by laughing. Many years ago, I read an article about a man who was told that he had a terminal illness. He accepted the fact that he was sick but believed that he could make himself well. In addition to following the treatment prescribed by his doctor, he designed a self-healing program that included vitamin C and lots of laughter. He watched funny movies and read joke books. He experienced a complete cure from his *seemingly* "incurable" illness.

Think about the last time you had a really good belly laugh; the kind where your laughter is totally uncontrollable. Remember how you felt afterward? If you're anything like me, you felt wonderful and probably giggled for days at whatever it was that was so funny. The same is also true for joy. Remember something that made you so completely happy that you grinned for months, just thinking about it.

Sadness will make you sick. Happiness will make you healthy. To experience how you unconsciously respond to these feelings, try this little experiment. Think of something sad and frown. Really notice how you feel and how your body responds. Now completely let go of that thought and feeling. Then remember something happy, funny, or joyful and smile. Again, really notice how you feel and how your body responds. Big difference, huh?

Your peace of mind is also important in promoting health. If you're sick or stressed, and you place yourself in an environment where you can experience harmony, it helps you clear yourself of negative thoughts and feelings. Letting go completely of all negativity and thinking positive thoughts can do wonders for you. Vacations and "getting away from it all" for a weekend are a great way to accomplish this, to give you a better perspective so you can change your perceptions.

But if your vacation isn't coming up for a while, there's another place you can go—right here, right now—that's always available to you. You can go into your nature scene, your peaceful place in your mind, at any time to experience and enjoy harmony. And there's another, very special healing place you can create in your mind—a Garden of Harmony—where you can experience the healing energies of sunlight and nature. Read through the following meditation, then close your eyes and be there.

Imagine yourself in a very beautiful garden. Looking around, you see lush, flowering bushes interspersed with open, spacious, grassy areas among many beds of beautiful flowers. Their fragrance is lovely and pleasing, and the purity of their colors is awe inspiring. As the bushes and flowers move gently in the soft, warm breeze, they create balance and beauty within the garden and within your mind. The garden emanates a vibrant feeling of energy, exuberant with life and health.

The day is filled with warm sunshine and a brilliant blue sky above you. The warmth of the sun on your body feels wonderful and rejuvenating. The green grass beneath your feet feels soft and luxuriant. The colors of the sky and the grass surround you, enveloping you with a soothing, peaceful feeling.

Everything in your garden vibrates in harmony, in tune with nature. It's quiet and peaceful, and the air is clean and pure. Breathing in, you sense the oneness of the garden with nature, and you feel peaceful within yourself as you begin to absorb the healing energies of the garden. As the warmth from the sun's rays begins to radiate through you, it fills you with a feeling of health and harmony. You feel perfectly in tune with nature and with the universal energies of sunlight.

Within your garden, you find a very special place of peace and harmony, where you feel most in tune with yourself and with the healing energies around you. As you enter this special place in your garden, inside your mind, you feel completely at peace with yourself and totally in harmony with the beauty and serenity all around you.

In this special healing place, center in on the warmth and light from the sun. Feel the vibrations of energy that are both around you and within you. Feel the healing energies of sunlight swirling and circling all around and through you. Breathe in the sunlight; breathe in the green-

ness and the health and harmony of this garden. Feel your mind—your thoughts and feelings—and your body vibrating in harmony with the light, completely in tune with your spiritual nature, completely in tune with the peaceful beauty of your garden, and enjoy the health and harmony you feel within yourself.

When you're done with this meditation, bring the inner peace and harmony and the radiant vibrations of health you've just experienced into your conscious mind and let them flow through your body over and over again. Allow this special Garden of Harmony to become a place of healing for you whenever you need it, or if you simply want to enjoy serenity and peace of mind.

MIND-POWER EXERCISES

1. Healing yourself from the inside out: To understand and heal the precipitating cause(s) for any dis-ease you may be experiencing, begin by looking at how it is currently expressing itself. Accept the sickness simply as it **is** in a loving, nonjudgmental way, knowing that the signs are there to help you heal yourself. Look for the symbology to help you trace it back to the originating situation and to the thoughts, feelings, and underlying beliefs that perpetuated the sickening experience.

When you see the originating belief, thought, or feeling, enter a meditative frame of mind to see how it began to physically manifest and to progress into what it is now. Look at it thoroughly so you can completely understand all aspects of it. You might want to view this on your Magical Mental Movie Screen and to surround yourself with the color of blue or green, or both, as you're doing this. The vibrations of blue will keep your thoughts calm and peaceful, and green will keep your feelings centered on health. Acknowledge your responsibility and reclaim your power.

Tell yourself that you're going to make yourself well and enlist the cooperation of both your conscious and your subconscious minds. Change your perceptions and previous beliefs. If necessary, change the energies of the previous event(s) that caused your sickness. Redirect and refocus the negative energy of your previous thoughts and feelings and their expression(s) into a positive awareness and a current reflection of healthy thoughts and feelings. Create what *can be*, which will soon become what *is*. Positively reprogram yourself to be completely and perfectly healthy. Put your new beliefs, feelings, and thoughts into action. Then watch health and harmony manifest first in your mind and then in your body.

2. Healing yourself from the outside in: If, for whatever reason, you're unable to see the cause (maybe it's lodged in your unconscious mind) then center your attention on the images of your illness. Look at the symbology of the symptoms to see what your sickness is saying to you. Use your imagination—the magical power of your mind—to help you read and see through the images. When you understand the message that your mind is giving you, work with that message and the images of your illness in the same way that you would work with the underlying cause(s), thoughts, beliefs, and feelings.

Accept the expressions of the sickness—the way that it is manifested—simply as they are, knowing that this is the way your body is helping you to heal yourself by showing you what to do for yourself. As you accept them in a loving, nonjudgmental way, you acknowledge your responsibility and reclaim your power. Enter a meditative frame of mind and tell yourself that you're going to make yourself well; you're going to heal yourself completely in body, mind, and spirit.

Change the images; change the way they're showing themselves. This gives both your body and your mind the message that you're now in the process of healing yourself, and your body will respond accordingly. Change the images so that they reflect health and harmony, rather than sickness and dis-ease. This will automatically and immediately begin to change your thoughts, feelings, and beliefs that created the sickness.

Just as in healing from the inside out, healing from the outside in will create what can be, which will soon become what is. As you continue to focus your attention on positive thoughts, feelings, and beliefs, and you direct your awareness on images of health, you'll see health and harmony manifest first in the images inside your mind and then in your body.

3. Put joy and laughter into your life on a continuous daily basis. Smile for no reason at all. Laugh a lot. Develop a great sense of humor. Negative situations all have their absurd, hilarious side. Look for it. See the humor and fun in everything. Most of all, just be happy. Your health depends on it.

CHAPTER THIRTEEN

The Essence of Energy

Everything is made up of energy, even you and the earth you walk on. Everything in nature is alive and filled with the joyous, vibrant energy of life. By exploring and experiencing the energy essence of all things, you'll understand the vibrations and expressions of many different forms of energies, and you'll expand your awareness to encompass the true reality of the world around you and within you.

Everything vibrates and resonates at varying frequencies of energy, depending on the life force or energy within it. A flower vibrates at a faster rate of energy than a rock. A situation or an experience vibrates to a different level of energy than a piece of furniture. Energy is in a constant flux and flow of motion, forever changing. The invisible energy essence within all things can be seen (sometimes

symbolically, sometimes literally), sensed, and felt on physical, psychic, and spiritual levels.

Auras are energy fields that surround every living thing.
You radiate energy from within. Inside your body, you
vibrate to the energies of rainbow colors. The vibrations
and expressions of that energy depend on your mood,
your attitude, your health, and your thoughts and feelings.
The energy is in continual motion, flowing in a pulsing,
rhythmic movement, like a wave or a heartbeat. It has
shape and form and density; it can be seen, felt, and sci-
entifically measured.

If you've ever noticed a halo around the moon or seen
sparkles of light shimmering from a raindrop, then you've
seen auras. While the halo may have been a gathering of
cosmic dust particles reflecting the light from the moon,
and the sparkles vibrating and shooting out from the raindrops may have been visible only when the sun was very
bright or when you looked at the raindrop from a certain
angle, you've seen the outer expression of the energy
within.

You can actually feel the vibrations of your aura with
your hands. Try this for yourself, but do it when you're
alone. If you do this in the company of other people, you'll
get some funny looks (unless they're reading this chapter
at the same time). Feel your aura around your head. It
might be helpful if you close your eyes to focus your sense
of touch. Place your hands about an inch away from your
head and slowly move them outward. You can feel where

your aura begins and ends. The feeling might be very slight and subtle at first until you become adept at feeling and sensing the vibrations of inner energies. You may experience a tingling sensation in your fingers or you might feel the waves of energy. You're feeling the outer expression of the energy that radiates from within you—the vibrations of your spiritual essence.

You can also feel the energies of something that exists only as a thought. Close your eyes and imagine a flower in front of you. Create it in your mind, then reach out and touch it in the same way that you felt your aura around your head. If you have trouble creating or feeling a flower, create a tree. A flower can be very delicate and detailed, but a tree is big and bold, and has a bigger aura.

What you've generated is a thought-form, and it is composed of invisible energy. Because you've seen it in your mind, it now exists—you've created it with the energy of your thought. In time, that flower or tree will manifest somewhere in some space in some reality.

Feeling intangible thought-forms may take a little bit of practice to start with, so we'll get back to it later, after it grows a bit. Let's begin with something you're already familiar with—something that's not physical or visible yet you know is very real. You know how to feel auras and sense invisible energy fields; you do it every day. When you first meet a person or see someone, you get an overall sense of what he or she is about and whether he or she is positive or negative. When you shake a person's hand, you can feel his or her vibrations. If you don't like that person, you'll instinctively pull away from his or her touch or move away from him or her. You may even experience some type of physical reaction, such as your body shaking or feeling cold, or you may experience some type of internal reaction, such as a sick feeling in the pit of your stomach or a sense of uneasiness.

If you like the person, you'll move closer to him or her without being consciously aware that you're doing this. You'll stand up straighter and your body will lean forward just a bit. This is because your energy fields are in harmony. You feel good when you're close to a positive energy field. You don't even have to touch or be touched by a person or be in the same room with him or her to feel and sense his or her vibrations. Just by thinking about someone, you pick up his or her vibrations.

Maybe you've had the experience of being in a room when someone who had a magnetic personality, or charisma, walked in. The minute this person entered, it seemed as if the room became charged with his or her energy. His or her aura/energy field was very strong, and if you liked his or her vibes, you felt drawn to him or her. If you didn't like his or her vibes, you probably bolted out of the room.

Relationships and interactions between people have energy fields. When two people's feelings for each other are very positive and loving, there's an interesting phenomenon that occurs. Their auras around their heads are joined in an arc effect, like a rainbow. If you're with these people, you can sense the caring they have for each other and it makes you feel good, whether you know them or not.

If you're arguing with someone, or if you're around someone who is sad or depressed, you instinctively want to get as far away from that person as you can because they drain your positive energy. Depending on the strength and intensity of another person's negativity and your reaction to that person, your energies can become depleted and diminished. However, if your energies are on the same wavelength, you'll feel quite comfortable with that person.

Places and situations also have energy fields. A positive place could be a person's home. When you walk in, you immediately pick up good vibes and you feel comfortable and relaxed there. A negative place could be a crowded store where you're literally bombarded with many different, and sometimes discordant, energies of the people there. You instinctively and unconsciously react by rushing through the store, wanting to get out of there, and you'll probably be in a bad mood for awhile afterward until your energy field becomes replenished and in tune with your own energies again.

Everywhere you go, you sense auras and energy fields, and you're influenced by unseen energies in a very real way. Every person in your life and every situation and place that you're in affects you, and you respond physically, psychically, mentally, and emotionally to those vibrations. The energies of your home and your workplace have a profound effect on you because of the amount of time you spend there.

Even energies of nature affect you dramatically. To me, a cloudy, snowy, cold day evokes negative feelings, although someone else may feel just the opposite. A barren landscape is depressing because of a lack of energy flowing through that area. A beautiful, sunny, warm day evokes positive feelings. A flower or a garden inspires a sense of harmony and peace.

Just as you're influenced by the energies around you, *you* influence energy on physical, psychic, and spiritual/universal levels by your thoughts, feelings, attitude, and actions. One of my students found a multipurpose way of dealing with people and situations that have a negative effect on him, as well as taking care of the blahs and replenishing his energy. It's a quick way to bring yourself up to a positive level and to change the vibrations of a situation or the way you're responding to another person. He also says it will neutralize negatives and in some cases will obliterate them altogether. And it does wonders for your health. He takes a deep breath and yells **"ENERGY"** at the top of his lungs. He instantly feels much more positive, not to mention completely energized. And everyone within earshot definitely gets a charge.

If you prefer to do things a bit more quietly and get the same results, envision yourself surrounded with the vibrant energies of white light as you simultaneously feel them within yourself. This clears and cleans the energy around you and replenishes your energy, as well as positively affecting the situation you're in or the person you're dealing with.

Unseen energies can accomplish very real things. You don't need to wait until after you've experienced something negative to change the energies. Surround yourself or a situation with white light before you experience anything that you know or sense might be unpleasant. People and situations respond very positively on many levels to this powerful energy. One of my students sent vibrations of white light to a coworker that she was having a lot of problems with to create a positive atmosphere between them. It worked so well that now they're very good friends.

Look a bit further into invisibility. Air is an invisible energy, yet it's very real and you couldn't live without it. What would you breathe? Even if you can't see something or touch it, it's still real and it exists and affects you in a tangible way.

You can become much more consciously aware of auras, unseen energy vibrations, and the energy essence within all living things by placing your full awareness into something or someplace and focusing your complete attention on it. *Mind projection* is projecting your awareness and your psychic sensitivity on wavelengths of energy. When you mind project, you're traveling on the invisible energies of your thoughts and feelings, and you're influencing and picking up the vibrations of a person, place, situation, or thing with your mind. This is not as abstract or as mind-boggling as it sounds. It's quite easy and you do it all the time.

Mind projection is similar to thinking about a memory. As you recall events from the past, you mind project your awareness on the energies of your thoughts and feelings into those past events. You're mind projecting and creating thought forms when you're thinking about or envisioning your plans and goals for the future or when you're thinking about someplace or someone and sending thought messages telepathically.

Another example is when you read a book or watch a movie and you become so involved with it that you feel as if you're there. You've mind projected your full attention and awareness into what you're reading or watching. Your attention on the images, thoughts, and feelings that the book or movie inspires in your mind can be so complete that you lose track of physical time and space, and it may feel as if you're in another world. (You are, even though your physical body isn't.)

The same is true for a daydream or a reverie. Close your eyes and imagine that you're sitting on a sandy beach on a warm summer day. See it with your mind's eye and feel it with all your senses. Become completely involved in the scene; focus all your awareness and attention into what you're seeing, sensing, and feeling. Be a participant, not an observer. Get emotionally involved. Don't pull up a memory; be there. Hear the splash of the waves and see them as they ebb and flow. Feel the warmth of the sand beneath your bare feet, the rays of the sun on your body, and the gentle breeze.

If you completely projected your consciousness into the beach scene, you may have begun to feel as if you were really sitting on a sandy beach on a beautiful summer day, instead of wherever you are now reading this book, and you may have even felt the warmth of the sun on your body or smelled the scent of suntan lotion or tasted the salt spray of the ocean. This is because the scene is so vivid and real in your mind that you began to physically respond to it, perhaps to the point where you actually experienced it in another level of your awareness. It was much more than a thought in your imagination or an image in your mind. When you mind project your complete awareness into something, you **are** experiencing it and your body responds accordingly. This may be very different from what you're used to experiencing in what you perceive to be your ordinary, waking, physical reality.

Mind projection is not limited by physical time, space, or matter. Only your physical body is limited to those. Your mind is completely free and will take you anywhere you want to go. You can mind project into any event, experience, or thing, into any place or situation, and into any time frame—past, present, or future—simply by projecting your awareness there. It's as easy as thinking a thought and wanting it to be so. As you open up and understand

your natural ability of mind projection, you become consciously aware of what you do all the time on a subconscious level.

Do a mini-mind projection to see for yourself what it's
like to travel through the invisible energies of time. Read
through the next two paragraphs, then project your awareness into a past and a future event. This gives you a frame-
work for projecting your consciousness into places,
situations, and things—for traveling into and through
unseen worlds of energy—and understanding how you
obtain information and filter it through your conscious
mind.

Project your awareness into an event that has already
occurred. Go back twenty-four hours and see what you
were doing. Don't reconstruct or recall the memory, simply allow your awareness to return to the past, a day ago
at this moment in time. Close your eyes for a moment and
be totally in the thoughts, feelings, and images in your
mind. If you completely mind project into the past, you
won't be recalling a memory. You'll actually reexperience
the occurrences in another vibration of energy and it will
be as real as it was the first time it happened.

Let go of the image, thought, and feeling and return to
the present. Be here, now, for a moment to get centered,
then mind project into the future, twenty-four hours from
now. See what you're doing; look for specific details rather
than generalities. Part of what you see might be based on

your expectations of what you plan to be doing. Go beyond that and allow yourself to pick up psychic information. If you truly project into the future, you'll instantaneously see and feel what you're doing, rather than searching your mind for an image.

Again, let go of the image, thought, and feeling and return to the present. Be here, now, for a moment to get centered. Write down your observations. Tomorrow, at this same time, be aware of what you experience and compare notes. Part of what you experience tomorrow will probably be influenced by what you saw and felt now, because even as you became aware of the events in that future moment, you also created and changed them.

Some people draw a blank on the future the first few times they try to project there. This happens because you're coming up against your belief that the future hasn't happened yet. Consider the concept that all of time is simultaneous, that everything is happening now in the same spaces but at different vibrations of energy at varying frequencies of motion. This concept can open up a whole new world for you. Just think of how you could change the future if it was happening now, if you could immediately see the consequences of your present actions as you think them—even before you do them.

Mind projecting through the vibrations of time and expanding your awareness into places, events, or situations can change your beliefs about time, space, and matter.

Traveling into and through the energies of both tangible and intangible things to sense their inner energy vibrations—their essence—might just change your concept of the world around you. Your ideas about reality may never be the same.

To see and experience things in a new light, enter a meditative frame of mind and explore the invisible energy vibrations of your favorite color. This is similar to what you did in Chapter Eight when you opened up your physical senses in a more aware, complete manner. Immerse yourself totally in this mind-opening meditation. *Be* the color and experience it in a unique way, with your five physical senses functioning together with your psychic senses in a heightened manner.

- To begin, think the thought of your favorite color—just the word. That's all you need to do. Your mind will draw an image of it for you and create a thought-form. Sense the aura around your favorite color, feeling it with your psychic senses and seeing it with your mind's eye. See and feel and sense how it vibrates—how it fluctuates and moves—and then mind project inside the energy vibrations of the color to pick up psychic information through your physical senses. See, feel, hear, taste, and smell the color with your mind. Notice your feelings—how you respond to the color and if and how your energies change.

- Picture your favorite color. See its intensity and brightness. Notice the shade and hue and tone. Is the color solid or is it open and airy? Does it fluctuate, seeming to come and go or to fade in and out, or is it still? What does the color really look like?
- Touch your favorite color. Feel the quality and texture of it. Does it feel like anything you've ever experienced before? Is it porous or solid? Heavy or light? Smooth or rough? Put it on and wear it. What does the color truly feel like?
- Listen to your favorite color. Hear the sounds it makes. Is it loud or quiet? Harmonious or discordant? Does it have a melody? Do you hear words or is it silent? What does the color sound like?
- Taste your favorite color. What flavor and texture does it have? Is it sweet or sour? Chewy or liquid? Crunchy or soft? Moist or dry? What does the color taste like?
- Smell your favorite color. Breathe in and experience the color. What aroma or scent does it have? Is the smell pleasant or offensive? Light or heavy? What does the color smell like?

Write down what you've experienced with your favorite color and how you perceive it now. Compare notes with your earlier description from Chapter One. Notice the difference. When you explored the color this time, you used your physical senses in a more aware, focused manner and you included your psychic perceptions of the color. You mind projected into its energy essence and you consciously centered all your attention into what you were experiencing to obtain information about the color.

Experiencing inner energies is magical and mystical. In the following mind-opening meditation—an awareness experience—you'll be exploring the life force and energies within a leaf and a stone. You'll be projecting your mind into these objects to obtain physical and psychic information about their individual energy essences. What you experience will help you in further opening up your psychic and sensory perceptions of everything around you, as well as enabling you to understand the inner energies that living, physical matter is comprised of.

This is easy to do. Have you ever noticed how a baby explores the world around him? He studies everything he finds thoroughly and with utter fascination. He uses all five physical senses to obtain information about the object. By doing this, the baby learns how the object fits into his world and what purposes it serves. I would even venture to say that he also understands the inner energies and outer vibrations of the object.

Every baby has explored a leaf and a stone; you've done it, too, but may have forgotten about it. Ask any mother or turn a crawling baby loose in a backyard and watch him for five minutes or less. He'll go straight for the leaf and the stone, probably because they're small and can be easily picked up and put in his mouth, or perhaps because the baby senses something magical inside them. So you're actually rediscovering something you already know everything about.

Pick a leaf from a plant or a tree—but not just any leaf. Look at the leaves and choose one that you feel drawn to, one that you sense would be right. Maybe touch several of them to become aware of their vibes. Before you pick the leaf, ask its permission. You may think this is silly or strange, but you'll understand why after you explore its energy essence. In your mind, imagine that you're talking to the leaf and ask permission to take it from the tree or plant. Explain your reasons; tell it why you want it. Listen quietly, and you'll become aware of some type of response or feeling from the leaf that will indicate whether or not you can pick it. Respect the answer that comes to you. If the leaf is willing to participate in your experiment, you'll get a sense that it's OK to use it. Be sure to say thank you. You are talking to a living thing that has its own feelings.

When you have the leaf, study it completely and thoroughly. View it with all the curiosity of something you're discovering for the very first time. Use your physical and psychic senses to find out all you can about it. Really see what it looks like and feels like. Touch it, caress it gently; feel its texture and its aura. Taste it; take a small bite of it or break it open and lick it. Smell it; breathe in its scent. Listen to it; hear the sounds it makes.

After you've gathered this outer information, hold the leaf gently in your hand. Touching or holding an object helps you tune into the vibrations of energy that are emitted from it, although it's not necessary to actually touch or hold an object to receive information about it. It's just a way to focus yourself. The impressions you receive through your physical sense of touching and your psychic sense of feeling will help you to become clearer about the energy within it.

Close your eyes, enter a meditative frame of mind, and experience the energy essence within this leaf. Go inside its energies and completely experience being inside it; gather all the information you can about it. Sense its vibrations with your mind. Take a journey—a magical, mystical mind trip—through the inner workings and feelings and energy vibrations of this leaf. Be the leaf. Explore and experience the life force and energy inside the leaf. Take your time with this; you'll be amazed at what this leaf can show you. When you're done, thank it, sprinkle it with water, and return the leaf to the earth so that it's touching the plant or tree where it came from.

To become aware of the difference in energy vibrations between this and other objects, do the same thing with a pebble. Even a stone has its energy essence and can show you many magical things. Before you pick it up from the ground, ask the stone if you can move it, promising to return it when you're through. Explore it with all your physical and psychic senses to experience what it's really like to be this stone, to be inside its energies. It's more alive than you might think it is. Discover and explore the inner vibrations and the energy that this rock emits. When you're done, thank the stone and return it to the earth.

By doing these mind-opening meditations and the following Mind-Power Exercises, you're exploring and experiencing both physical and nonphysical realms and dimensions of energy and matter on many levels of your awareness. This helps you to achieve an understanding of their interrelationship. You're becoming more aware of unseen energies and the energy essence of all things, as well as understanding the inner and outer vibrations of the world around you. With the knowledge you acquire, you can use invisible energies to help you in every aspect of your life, as well as rediscovering your true spiritual essence and exploring the universe within your mind.

MIND-POWER EXERCISES

1. Become more aware of energy fields that you come in contact with every day. Travel into and through the energies of places and situations. Notice how you respond to the vibrations and how your thoughts and feelings affect and influence the energies.

2. Take mind trips through time, space, and matter. Explore where your mind takes you. This will help you discover many magical, mystical secrets and your true power

in creating your own reality. Just remember that thoughts are tangible things and that you create your reality from the inside out.

3. Mind project into and experience the energies of many different kinds of objects, such as a key, a piece of plastic, a slice of fruit, etc. This will help you understand different levels and vibrations of energy.

4. Reexperience the colors of the rainbow and the objects you first became aware of in the rainbow meditation from Chapter One. Go inside the colors and the objects and explore their energy essence. Notice how much better you understand them now.

5. Mind project inside your physical body. Explore it from within and see what your energies are all about. You may be surprised at what your body shows you and tells you.

6. If you feel adventuresome, mind project inside your mind. I guarantee you'll be awed.

7. Explore and experience the energy essence of things in nature, such as sunshine, rain, trees, clouds, flowers, a real rainbow, the air you breathe, etc. Then go into the energies of the earth to see what the earth shows you and to understand what the earth is all about.

8. Hug a tree every day. It will make you feel good and the tree will love it. Plant a tree in your yard. If you live in an apartment, plant one in a park or arrange to have a tree planted in a rain forest or another natural setting. Name it after yourself and watch it grow as it spreads its roots into the earth and the branches reach toward the universe. Every once in a while sit underneath it and meditate; listen to the secrets of nature that it shares with you.

Maybe this tree is the same tree you created at the beginning of this chapter! Do you think that's possible? And what about the flower? Is it growing somewhere, perhaps in a Garden of Harmony? Are they real? Are they tangible and touchable? Or do they exist only in your mind? Now that you know about invisible energies, what do you think?

CHAPTER FOURTEEN

Enlightenment and Empowerment

Sunrises hold a promise of a new and wonderful discovery, the dawn of a new beginning, the dawn of a new light beginning to grow within you. Perhaps you're ready to explore and experience the light within yourself as you travel in your mind beyond the spectrum of the sunrise. You're ready to completely remember the magical power of your mind and to rediscover the mystical awareness of your soul.

Imagine . . .

It's only moments before dawn. It's a beautiful summer morning and you're outside, enjoying the beginning of a new day. You feel a gentle, warm breeze and smell the fresh scent of the morning air. You hear birds chirp-

*ing in the distance and the sound is muted and pleasant
as they welcome the dawn of a new day.*

*Looking around, you see a few trees and the ground is
covered with grass. You feel like taking off your shoes and
walking barefoot in the grass. It feels like velvet beneath
your feet, and as you walk, you feel free and happy, enjoying the beginning of a brand-new day.*

*Listening to your thoughts and watching their images
move in your mind, you remember when you walked
through the forest and reconnected with yourself—with
your true spiritual nature—and you rediscovered the harmony of the earth with the universe. You remember the
tree that told you the secrets of nature—the secrets of your
soul—telling you that the universe is within yourself. You
remember the wonderful waterfall that created rainbows
everywhere. When you looked into the quiet pool beneath,
you saw both your physical self and your spiritual self
mirrored together in the water, and you became aware of
how the earth is a mirror of the universe, just as you are
a physical mirror of your spiritual self.*

*As you continue to walk, listening to your thoughts,
you know that there's a beach nearby because you can
hear the sound of the waves, and you think you'd enjoy
the sunrise even more if you were at the beach. You begin
to walk toward the beach and now you can feel the sand
beneath your feet; it feels pleasantly warm and cushions
you as you walk.*

Sitting on the beach and watching the waves as they gently touch the shore, you feel a wonderful sense of peace and harmony within yourself and all around you. Listening to the ebb and flow of the tide relaxes you completely. Breathing in deeply, you feel perfectly content, at one with yourself and with the earth and the universe.

Looking up at the sky, you have a clear view of the horizon as the water seemingly touches the sky. You see a few clouds just above the horizon, and you notice that they're tinged with the early colors of dawn. Pale orange at first, then the pale orange blends into a beautiful mixture of coral and pink. It's almost as if pearls are coloring the bottom of the clouds, or maybe the water is reflecting the color of the sunrise onto the clouds. The beauty and clarity of the colors inspire a sense of awe and wonderment inside you as you realize that you're seeing the colors of dawn, the colors of a new day, the colors of a new beginning.

You notice that the sky is getting lighter and lighter. As the light from the sun begins to shine behind the clouds, you see the first rays of the sunrise begin to come over the horizon, and the light is reflected and mirrored on the water. The light of this sunrise vibrates with a wonderful feeling of energy and awareness, and you sense that this sunrise is very special; it's magical. Turning your face up to the sun, you breathe in the light.

The warmth and light of the sun envelops you as you breathe it inside your mind and your body. It fills your

*entire body and your mind with pure energy and aware-
ness, gently touching every nerve, every muscle, and every
fiber of your body. You can feel your body and your mind
vibrating in harmony with the warmth and light of the
sun, with the energy of awareness. As you feel and sense
the sunrise with every part of you, you feel drawn into
the sunrise, knowing that you're ready to completely rediscover the magical, mystical power of your mind, ready to
reawaken your spiritual awareness.*

*The early colors of dawn begin to change into the
golden color of the sun. Somewhere within yourself, you
realize that you are the colors of dawn. You are the colors of the sunrise. Just as the water reflected the early colors of dawn onto the clouds, you know that the sunrise
in the universe—mirrored within your mind—is a reflection of your spiritual awareness and knowledge, opening
up within you, reawakening you to the power within
yourself.*

*The sunlight sparkles and shimmers on the water,
reflecting the light of the universe. As you center your
awareness into the sunrise, it becomes brighter and
brighter, illuminating every part of your mind, filling your
mind with pure enlightenment. You know that the sunrise is within you and that you are the sunrise.*

*The sun is above the horizon now, and as the sun con-
tinues to rise in the sky, you rise with it—higher and
higher. The feeling is exhilarating and you feel more alive
and awake and aware than you've ever felt before.*

There's a special place that you know of, a magical place that you've just remembered is beyond the colors of dawn, beyond the spectrum of the sunrise. As you go into and through and beyond the light of the sunrise, you enter that special and most magical place within yourself, within your mind. It feels as if you're coming home, as if you're returning to yourself. You know you've been here before in this sacred place inside your soul. You've always known the way to this most special and magical place.

And now you see that the sun is beginning to rise in the center of your mind and you know that you're completely opening up the power of your mind, the power of your spiritual awareness. As you become more aware of your true spiritual essence, a pure white light—a light brighter than the sunrise—enters into every part of your mind. You notice how the light vibrates around you and you feel how it vibrates within you. You begin to feel this light, this magical energy of spiritual knowledge vibrating inside you—inside your body, your mind, and your soul. You experience a sensation of awe and wonder and joy as you completely open yourself up and allow this empowering energy of spiritual awareness and enlightenment to enter inside of you.

This pure white light opens your awareness to the truth of your spiritual essence and knowledge. As the light becomes brighter and brighter within you, you become more and more aware of your inner spiritual knowledge—

knowledge that is infinite and goes beyond what words can describe.

You know that this light is the light of your soul—the light of the universe. And you know that this is the same light you first saw above the rainbow—the light that shimmered through the mist and sparkled with the energy essence of the universe. You remember how you gathered it all around you and breathed it inside you. You remember how you became part of the light—the light that shines within you—as you absorbed it within your body and your mind and your soul. Breathe in the light again. Become the light and be the light.

*As you breathe in the pure and positive energy of the light and you fully absorb the spiritual energy within yourself, you know that your spiritual enlightenment is completely opening up inside of you as you become more aware and awake than ever before. As you accept the light that is radiating from within the sunrise, from within the center of your being—your soul—you become fully aware of your true spiritual nature and you know that **you are the universal essence of light that shines upon the earth.***

The light within you becomes brighter as the sun continues to rise. Your spiritual knowledge and the awareness of your true nature is interwoven with the rays of sunshine, with the colors of a new day, a new beginning. Your inner awareness becomes clearer and brighter at every moment, as you experience and enjoy the sunrise, as you experience enlightenment within your mind.

Enjoy and explore the light within you as you redis-cover your true spiritual essence and you completely open up the magical, mystical power of your mind.

You see a golden sun ray that emanates from the sun-rise, a golden sun ray that emanates from you. You notice how the sun ray originates from the sun and from you, and how it travels from its source to gently touch the earth and to light the way of a beautiful new day. You notice that this sun ray sparkles on the water and shines on the beach where you watched the dawn begin, where you enjoyed the beginning of the sunrise. Become part of that golden sun ray and travel with it onto the beach where you watched the dawning of the light within you.

And now you're sitting on the beach again and you see that the sun is completely above the horizon, above the clouds. The colors are different now; the clouds that reflected the early colors of dawn now reflect the color of gold—the color of the sun and the color of knowledge. The sky is a very bright blue, and even as you look at the clouds that are golden, they change to a pure white, as if they've absorbed the light of the sunrise.

You look over the water and notice how the sunlight sparkles and shimmers, mirroring and reflecting the light from the sun. And you know that the white light of the universe—the light of your soul—shines brightly within you.

You feel the warmth of the sun and the gentle breeze. You smell the scent of the morning air and hear the sound *of birds chirping in the distance as they welcome the sunshine. You smile up at the sun, knowing that you've remembered the secrets of your soul and rediscovered your spiritual knowledge within yourself on the journey you've just taken beyond the spectrum of the sunrise.*

Remembering the magical power of your mind and rediscovering the mystical awareness of your soul is the dawn of a new beginning, a promise of many new and wonderful adventures and discoveries. Your awareness of your spiritual knowledge and the power of your mind is reflected and mirrored in every experience you have as you explore this path that you're traveling—a magical, mystical path in your mind and in your life—a rainbow path.

As you continue upon this path, many treasures and rewards open up to you with every step you take. Spiritual knowledge is the most wonderful treasure of all, because you can allow this knowledge to lead you to the true awareness of who you are and to self-empower you to express your magical, mystical mind power in all your thoughts, feelings, and experiences.

My sincere wish for you is a lifetime filled with joy and happiness, wonder and awe. Travel lightly on your rainbow path.

About the Author

Gloria Chadwick is a teacher turned full-time writer. She enjoys thunderstorms (the power of the universe is awesome!), walking barefoot though the rain, and searching the sky for rainbows. She hugs trees regularly and grows prizewinning gardens. She also enjoys sitting on the beach in Hawaii watching sunrises, but since she lives in Chicago with her two daughters, she does that mostly in her mind.

Currently she is working on *Looking into Your Future Lives* (forthcoming October 1996), which is a sequel to *Discovering Your Past Lives*, published by Contemporary Books.

She has also written a New Age novel, *Somewhere Over the Rainbow: A Soul's Journey Home*, published by Mystical Mindscapes. Based on a past life, the story is part fact, part fiction. It offers an entertaining adventure through this earth experience that we call life as it takes a lighthearted look at the reality of reincarnation and the ups and downs of being spiritual in a physical world.